A LIFE POST-PARTUM

My Journey Through Postpartum Depression

LISA HARDWICK

Copyright © 2020 by Lisa Hardwick. All rights reserved.

This book or any portion thereof may not be reproduced or used in any manner whatsoever without the express written permission of the publisher except for the use of brief quotations in a scholarly work or book review. For permissions or further information contact Braughler Books LLC at:

info@braughlerbooks.com

The views and opinions expressed in this work are those of the author and do not necessarily reflect the views and opinions of Braughler Books LLC.

cover photo: kzww/Shutterstock.com

Printed in the United States of America

Published by Braughler Books LLC., Springboro, Ohio

First printing, 2020

ISBN: 978-1-970063-72-1 soft cover
ISBN: 978-1-970063-73-8 ebook

Library of Congress Control Number: 2020914347

Ordering information: Special discounts are available on quantity purchases by bookstores, corporations, associations, and others. For details, contact the publisher at:

sales@braughlerbooks.com

or at 937-58-BOOKS

For questions or comments about this book, please write to:

info@braughlerbooks.com

Contents

Chapter 1: History 3

Chapter 2: Pregnant 15

Chapter 3: Labor 23

Chapter 4: The First Week 37

Chapter 5: Sick 49

Chapter 6: April Eighth 63

Chapter 7: Breast is Best 75

Chapter 8: Help 79

Chapter 9: Emergency 89

Chapter 10: Grandma Hardwick 97

Chapter 11: Lies 105

Chapter 12: The Doctors .111

Chapter 13: New Moms 119

Chapter 14: June Journals 127

Chapter 15: July 131

Chapter 16: Vacation 139

Chapter 17: Fall 147

Chapter 18: Christmas 157

Chapter 19: Spring 163

Where Are They Now? 171

Faith. 175

Resources 177

References 179

About the Author 181

Dear reader,

This is the story of my first year as a mother.

It's wild.

I was diagnosed with severe postpartum depression and postpartum anxiety, mental health disorders that affect up to one in seven new mothers[1].

Too many new mothers believe in the lie that they are the only ones who struggle to survive a time of life that is *supposed* to be so full of happiness and joyful moments with their new baby. I want to do something about that. They need to know the truth. I want to tell them that they are not alone.

I have been there.

It's so dark, isn't it?

Let me bring you some light. We can get through this, but we have to stick together.

Are you ready?

Here we go!

CHAPTER 1
History

To the woman He said,
"I will greatly multiply your pain in childbirth,
in pain you will bring forth children;"
Genesis 3:16a (NASB)

This pain of childbirth has been known for thousands of generations.

In pain we weep alone after the news of another miscarriage, ashamed of a body which will not respond to our greatest efforts or our longest prayers. In pain we cry out as the contractions steal our breath, sweat pours into our bloodshot eyes, the hours press on. In pain we lay in the darkness of our solitude, the postpartum depression consumes our minds beyond the point of reality. In pain we hide the story of a stillborn, trusting no one else to share in our grief which will never truly end. In pain we mourn the loss of our identities as the nursing baby steals hour after hour of sleep, each sunrise we acknowledge another day of sacrifice. In pain we grow bitter as the years pass with no conception, despite every needle, pill, and procedure we were promised would finally work.

In pain we push others away.

Only in love can we share our own pain with others. Only in love will we fall on each other's shoulders, helpless under a burden much too heavy for one woman to carry. It is love that allows us to admit our weaknesses, to accept help, to come alongside the generation of women who will rise up after us and show them how to bring light to those lost in the darkness.

In love, I tell my story.

. . .

I met Noah at a lasagna party my freshman year of college. We were married less than two years later.

Noah fascinated me. He could always make me laugh. We had mutual friends and entered into the "friendly acquaintance" zone. I knew he loved Jesus and so did I. We went to different universities, but we ran into each other during weekend adventures. He knew how to build a bonfire, and he also knew how to be a gentleman. He wore band T-shirts and baseball caps. He had a deep voice and broad shoulders. He liked loud music and loud colors. He knew no strangers. He liked what he liked, and he wasn't concerned about anyone's opinions.

We became friends.

Then we became best friends.

We spent hours together on the phone most days. He left me long voicemails with jokes and songs that I could listen to on my break at work. We threw a tea party for our friends at Centennial Park in downtown Nashville. Everyone had to bring their own fancy cup and saucer for a spot of tea. He cooked us pancakes for movie nights at the student apartment he shared with three roommates. He was from a land far away which he called "Ohio." I had never visited his homeland and could barely point it out on a map. Anything north of Kentucky was a mystery to me. It sounded cold. We talked and talked and talked until it seemed like we knew everything about each other.

We went to the same church, which was a small assembly of misfits who were tattooed, pierced, and passionate for Jesus. It was awesome. Noah, me, and a half dozen other church members spent Saturday afternoons with the homeless community in the city. We packed lunches, listened to life stories, and developed friendships with our neighbors who didn't have the luxury of a permanent address. I watched Noah during those moments and saw how he never hesitated to hug those who longed for comfort. He cried with the person who needed someone to cry with. He spoke to the person who everyone else ignored. He sought out the lonely and the outcast and embraced them like family.

I didn't mean to, but I fell in love.

One night we took the half mile walk from Noah's student apartment to the geographical center of the state of Tennessee, which is marked by a stone obelisk that local college students often vandalized with graffiti and/or urine. There was nothing romantic about this particular spot. We walked so slow, because we had so much to say to each other. We never wanted our conversations to end. When we turned around to walk back, something sparked between us. It was electric. I wanted to be with him. Forever. I never wanted to leave him. I couldn't imagine my days without him. I knew I loved him.

Noah moved close enough to me that his hand brushed mine. We both smiled and looked at each other. We took a few more steps in silence, and then he held my pinky in his. We didn't say anything. Finally, after months of long conversations, we both had nothing to say. It was ridiculously adorable. He walked me to my car, and he hugged me. He said we fit together like puzzle pieces, and I agreed. He didn't let go, and I was glad. I wanted to stay in that one moment forever. It was the perfect fit.

We were engaged after six months of dating, and we were married six months after our engagement. We just knew. We loved the Lord, and His grace became the foundation to our relationship. Our hearts beat to the same drummer. We were idealistic and wanted to change the world. I was twenty years old to his twenty-two. Friends and family suggested I wait to get married until I had finished school, but I didn't want to listen. Our wedding was in July after my sophomore year of college.

Noah had graduated that spring. He was offered a paid internship that would begin in the fall, and my source of income at the time was from a part-time position as a swim coach. On the drive home from our honeymoon, Noah received a call that the internship position had been eliminated. Budget cutbacks. It was 2008, and the recession hit us before we had the chance to open our wedding presents. My newlywed husband got three part-time jobs in the months that followed and drove a red 1998 Pontiac Grand Am that leaked mysterious liquids at the most inopportune times. Our apartment sat in a neighborhood that resonated with gunshots and sirens. I rode the bus to school early in the mornings and stayed late to study and coach. Once a week we treated ourselves to one item each from the Taco Bell $1 menu for "date night." If it was a good week, we split a soda.

I didn't want to admit to anyone that I was drowning. I was not a stranger to anxiety and depression. During high school, I had developed bulimia as a means to cope with the unrealistic expectations of perfection I assigned myself. By then I was a straight-A student and a talented athlete, but I was a slave to my own addiction to achievements. I found my identity in what I accomplished, and I never seemed to accomplish enough. I was diagnosed with clinical depression at fifteen and treated with prescription medications for years. As a college student, the bulimia lessened in frequency but continued to be my means to cope with stress.

During the first year of marriage, I tried to keep up my pace, but my body reacted. I started to experience frequent panic attacks at school that landed me on the ground, dizzy and breathless. I was nauseated. I had bouts of insomnia. I could hardly open my mouth without shooting pain in my jaw. My primary care doctor prescribed an antidepressant to help with the symptoms. It was a bandage that only covered up the deeper issue. I spent a few sessions with a therapist with whom I couldn't seem to relate, and I quit going.

I found myself bingeing and purging more as the stress of school, finances, and newlywed life continued. I took diet pills on long days. I started running five days a week and drinking on the other two. We stopped attending church, and we began to serve ourselves entirely. Every free moment and free dollar were spent to make ourselves look good and feel good. I shoved myself into performance mode and took on extra classes. I smiled and nodded and looked fine from the outside; I made sure of that. I graduated *summa cum laude* a semester early.

I was miserable.

I worked in insurance after graduation and immediately fell in love with the corporate environment. It was competitive, and I knew how to compete. Noah had also secured a full-time job, and our hearts turned from humility to pride. Money was the new goal, not service to the Lord or compassion for His people. We grew comfortable and stagnant. We replaced the Pontiac for two newer vehicles, secured an apartment in a safer area of town, and added a miniature Schnauzer, Tulip, to our crew. We didn't seek the Lord, we sought status. I was on a hamster wheel of performance, but began to lose any sense of purpose or meaning in the madness. Everything appeared to be going according to *my* plan, but somehow I was never *quite* good enough.

Or smart enough.

Or thin enough.

Or witty enough.

We all have our lists.

"I'm going to go inside and shoot myself in the head with the shotgun," I cried on the phone to Noah as I drove up to our empty apartment late one Saturday night. I was twenty-three and drunk.

He kept me on the phone, as he had always managed to do. He raced home. He sat in the passenger seat of my little blue Honda and I cried on his shoulder until I fell asleep. The next day the shotgun was gone, as were the knives, razors and pills. Noah made the hard choice to show tough love as we sat at the kitchen table and he asked me to take time off of work and pursue intensive treatment for depression. I knew it was the right decision, but that did not mean I was happy about it. I agreed because I loved him. He was my best friend. I met with a therapist three times per week as well as a psychiatrist who prescribed heavy doses of antidepressant and anti-anxiety medications. I took a three-month leave of absence from work and slept for fifteen to eighteen hours a day, sedated from the medications. I didn't acknowledge God in these circumstances. I was just angry.

I didn't believe I could ever find relief from bulimia, but slowly the mental health professionals pulled off the onion layers of my mind to find the root cause. It was messy. After two years of treatment, relapses, mistakes, and tiny victories, I began to treat my body with respect. I started to lift weights instead of hours of endurance sports. I sought strength instead of skinny.

I put God out of my mind during this time, and I awarded myself all the credit for my recovery. I continued to seek money, status, and good feelings. Once I was in a healthier state, I began to search for a change of scenery. A fresh start. I applied for a job that doubled my salary, but required full-time travel and a cross-country move.

I interviewed and was offered the position. We moved to Des Moines, Iowa after I had lived in Tennessee for twenty-five years. Sixty-hour work weeks with full-time travel began immediately, and I spent two hundred and fifty-five days in a hotel the first year of work. Our marriage didn't benefit from such a sudden shift, but I valued my paycheck more than anyone else. We both served money and the deceitful sense of security that it brought. Although the past mental health treatment had given me beneficial tools to deal with the inevitable stressors of life, anxiety and depression became unmanageable after two years on the road. I didn't believe there was a God who would want to hear from me in this mess, so I began to drink by myself and cut my wrists. My desire was not for suicide, but the act of self-harm became addicting. Once again, I did not want to admit I was drowning.

I applied for different jobs that did not require travel, but each opportunity ended with a closed door. Rejected. Rejected. Rejected. I felt stuck in the middle of the cornfields of Iowa in what seemed to be a perpetual hangover. I thought I had made a good choice to support our family financially, but the situation seemed to be a big mistake that I couldn't undo. One night in a hotel in Phoenix, Arizona I polished off half a bottle of vodka, and then sat in the bath, absentmindedly cutting divots into my wrists. After the shame of what I had done hit me, I dried off and wrapped myself in a towel. When I turned around and saw myself in the mirror, I was shocked to see who I had become.

I realized then that I could either keep going and end up dead, or I could admit I needed help. Lots of help.

I revealed my habits to Noah, and he flew to Arizona to see me. We decided that I would resign from my job and we would move to Ohio to be near his family. We didn't know what we would do for work, but we agreed we had to make a big change. We didn't know where we would live, so Noah's mother offered us their basement until we could get settled in the area. I anticipated staying with them for a month, *maybe* two, but the Lord had very different plans. I interviewed for an office job in Cincinnati. It offered me a 60% pay cut and a heavy workload of negotiating injury settlements with angry customers over the phone. I took it. We moved into my in-law's windowless, half-finished basement, bringing the total house population to six people, three dogs, and one cat.

Noah found a part-time job, but with our total income cut in half, we ate through our savings despite having a free roof over our heads. I began to exercise and diet to the extreme once again. Old habits reappeared. I called myself an agnostic. I lost hope in a loving God who works all things together for my good. I didn't see a point in living. I had no purpose.

Noah's very first client worked at a church that just so happened to be a block from our in-law's house. She invited us to church, and I declined. She invited us again, and I declined. The third time she asked us to visit, I agreed to go sit through a service so she would leave us alone. We arrived at the church late and sat in the back row. I don't know what songs were played or what sermon was given, but within minutes of sitting down, the Holy Spirit broke me to pieces. A holy repentance filled my mind, opening my eyes once again to the things unseen. I looked back on the past six years of wandering, lost in a Sinai wilderness of depression and destruction. I cried out in my spirit to the Lord, "I'm so sorry! I'm so sorry! What have I done?! Have I ruined my life, my future? Have I ruined everything!?"

> "The Lord is merciful and gracious, slow to anger and abounding in steadfast love.
> He will not always chide, nor will he keep his anger forever.
> He does not deal with us according to our sins, nor repay us according to our iniquities."
> Psalm 103: 8-10 (ESV)

I realized that God had not been silent during this journey, but I had let pride and fear keep me from hearing his faithful voice guiding me back to His presence. Perhaps He had to get me down into the basement so I would finally sit still and listen. I had lived for the approval of people, for wealth, and I thought nothing of serving the needs of others. The Holy Spirit blew the dust off of my mind, and the foundational knowledge of the Gospel that had taken root in my soul from a young age came back to me. I saw clearly once again. I had made things so complicated instead of following the greatest commandment to simply love the Lord and love others. The Lord reminded me that this call to love with all of my being was my sole aim in life.

The office job I had was with a company that I began to realize did not value justice or integrity in the workplace. Once the Holy Spirit took over again in my soul, I became conflicted and anxious in my decision-making. I knew I couldn't show the love of God and His mercy without risking my professional reputation. However, I was afraid to leave a job that provided benefits and a reliable paycheck. Each day I returned, it became more and more clear that the Lord was calling me elsewhere, to an entirely different path. Noah found a job opening for me to be a part-time swim coach for young swimmers making nine dollars an hour with no benefits. *"This is your new job,"* I heard the Holy Spirit whisper. To love the children, to teach the children, to learn humility and graciousness all over again.

I went to work the next day and resigned with a three-day notice. It felt like jumping off a cliff. On paper, this decision would not work. In my Spirit, there was "the peace which surpasses all understanding" (Philippians 4:7).

I couldn't stop smiling on my first day back at the pool to coach. I started to laugh again. I learned to think simply. I did not realize the darkness of the pit I had been in until I began to see the light. I secured a second part-time job in the produce section of Whole Foods. I worked with my hands and learned to respect food once again. I regained the capacity for love, to show compassion and mercy. My marriage blossomed, and we began to serve again within the body of Christ. We worked with high school students. Life suddenly had meaning and purpose again. To love, to love, to love.

God let us stay in my in-law's basement for eighteen months so we could learn the lesson of humility. I wanted the lesson to end quickly, but perhaps I am a slow learner. I no longer had a professional job title, any expendable income, nor a living space I could call my own. Noah juggled three part-time jobs during that season, but he also found a peace within the madness as the Lord steadily provided. Prior to this time, we had no desire to have children. Zero. It was not in our game plan. We were content to be the fun uncle and the aunt who diligently took her birth control pills. God again had different plans. Better plans with perfect timing. After our eighteen-month lesson in humility, God gave us a one-bedroom apartment that was the perfect size for Noah, me, and little Tulip.

I caught baby fever, and it was contagious. We decided we wanted to try for a baby, but for the safety of the pregnancy, I needed to come off of the Cymbalta prescription I had been taking for the past five years. My primary care doctor worked with me through a sixth-month withdrawal process. He offered alternative prescription medication that was considered safe for a growing fetus, but I refused. I told myself that I no longer needed any medication to treat depression or anxiety, that I had enough tools to manage symptoms without any professional help. We decided I would plan to stay at home with our child instead of returning to work, so that I could raise her in a home we prayed would be full of love. I assumed I would have all the time in the world to take care of myself.

CHAPTER 2
Pregnant

Growing a baby is hard!

When I saw the positive sign on the pregnancy test, I called Noah and asked him to come home. I wrote *"Big Sister"* on a scarf for Tulip to wear to announce it to him. He drove home in record time. When he saw the scarf and realized I was pregnant, we were both overwhelmed and fell to our knees on the faux wood linoleum in our little kitchen. We told the Lord that we would dedicate our child's life to Him.

I had beautiful moments in the process, and I cried my fair share of happy tears. I fell in love with my husband all over again as I saw his reaction to my burgeoning bump. He began a relationship with his daughter before she was even the size of a plum. He sang to her through my belly, his deep voice was one she learned as quickly as her ears could develop. He told her things he wanted her to know: she was loved, she was wanted, she would never be alone. He provided her a good selection of music and explained each piece as he placed the earbuds on either side of my belly button. She liked Johnny Cash the most. That tiny baby had rhythm.

When I first heard the heartbeat, the doctor declared, "This one is a mover and a shaker!"

I laughed until I cried, blown over with thanksgiving. At 19 weeks pregnant, we arrived for the first ultrasound. As soon as the image of our child lit up the screen Noah cried the same type of tears that I saw at the end of our wedding aisle nearly ten years ago; that man was head over heels in love. We had both hoped for a daughter, and when the technician announced, "It's a girl!" Noah bent over and wept into the towel I had used to wipe off the extra gel from my stomach. I laughed through the rest of the ultrasound, and the technician told us we were the most enthusiastic new parents she had ever met.

Each evening we prayed the same prayer for her: "Thank you Lord for a healthy, strong, wise individual who will be a world changer for the Gospel."

I wanted everything for my daughter to be pink; it's my favorite color. I wanted everything to be pink with flowers, lace, and bows. Everything was soft, and everything was pretty.

I asked the people I trusted, "if you could only give one piece of parenting advice, what would it be?"

The initial reaction was almost always, "Just *one*?!"

Yep. Just one big one. I kept my favorites.

"Don't beat yourself up over the little stuff. Find the small victories, the little things that you accomplish, and really celebrate them."

"Pray. A lot."

"Learn to laugh at yourself now. Don't take things so seriously, that's half the battle."

"It's never too early to read books to your children. They may not understand the words, but they learn to love the experience."

"It's O.K. to step away when you need a moment to breathe. Babies will cry and cry and cry. God made them cute for a reason. Sometimes you just need a moment to step away and take a breath."

"Accept all of the help that you are offered."

Pregnancy brought on a fatigue unlike anything I had experienced in the past. Bodily resources were being rerouted to the tiny chickpea in my uterus, and I could hardly keep my eyes open during the first trimester. I wanted to love pregnancy. I wanted to be one of the unicorn women who feel most alive while their baby is growing within, but I just felt exhausted. I cried easily. I continued to work both part-time jobs which forced me to stay moving, regardless of how much I complained about my feet hurting. I worked out up until my due date. Exercise kept my mind strong. I wanted to be as physically prepared for labor as I could be.

I ate toast with peanut butter and banana every afternoon. That was one craving that never got old. I sat on the couch and watched *The Office* more times than I'd like to admit, especially during the last month of pregnancy. I knew my free time would soon be slashed to a minimum, so I wanted to enjoy it while I had it. I slept poorly and woke up every couple hours to a needy bladder and a sore back. I was told this was nature's way of getting me accustomed to less sleep. I loved to wear maternity clothes, especially on Thanksgiving.

I was quite an emotional pregnant lady. Like the time I stood in front of an empty rotisserie chicken display at the grocery store and cried. I really wanted some chicken. The store advertised these birds on sale at $5.00 each! It was a great deal! My pregnant emotions could not handle the disappointment. Pregnancy brain was a real thing too. Like the Saturday morning in December I locked my keys in my car at the Target parking lot. I was supposed to be at work in ten minutes, and we were in the middle of a snow storm. Noah was a convenient thirty minutes away. Good thing I wore sneakers, not snow boots. That was a fun day.

Although I had been through extensive treatment and counseling for my past eating disorder, I still feared the inevitable pounds that would appear during pregnancy. Logically, I knew that adequate weight gain was essential for growing a baby, but I still battled my old mindset to restrict and control food during this time of uncertainty. The internet told me not to gain any weight during the first trimester, so I didn't. The obstetrician told me to quit looking at the internet about pregnancy, so I did. Perhaps that was actually the best piece of parenting advice.

I gained eight pounds during my fourth month, so I stopped looking at the scale.

Postpartum depression was discussed with me every visit to the obstetrician because of my history with mental health issues. I assumed the role of an ostrich and stuck my head underground. The transition to parenthood was intimidating enough, and the thought of experiencing postpartum depression after giving birth was too scary to think about. I told myself it wouldn't happen; I told myself it would be different.

Our one-bedroom apartment was a third story walk-up, and the stairs became more of a challenge as each month passed. I organized baby clothes and baby gear into a corner of our closet. We didn't have enough room to assemble a crib, so we planned for the baby to sleep in her Pack-n-Play until we were able to move to a bigger space. I was primarily focused on preparing myself for the "full body marathon" of labor. I was determined to have a natural birth. The thought of my spinal cord being punctured by an epidural was scarier than the thought of pain.

I purchased *The Bradley Method's* learning material. I went through all the books twice, and I learned everything I possibly could about the birthing process. I could recite the stages of birth and all the acrobatic miracles my cervix was about to perform. I did my daily relaxation techniques and the one thousand Kegels exactly as the *The Bradley Method* suggested. I began to look down on people who chose an epidural or a scheduled C-section. I thought "they must just be weak-minded. I would *never* do that. I'm going to do it the *right* way. My way."

• • •

March 14th, my due date, came and went. I wasn't surprised. I had been warned that going beyond a due date is common with a first pregnancy. I had taken my walks, eaten my spicy foods, bounced on balls, had sexy time with my husband, squatted and stretched and prayed that the baby would make her appearance. I thought, "It's okay. I've stayed in shape. I'm fine. The doctor will let me go two more weeks and it's sure to happen before then. *I will refuse to be induced.*"

Noah and I went to my appointment the following day, and I was nervous. My blood pressure was high. In fact, it was the second week that it was high. "Dangerously high," I was told. I cried. I asked them if it could be due to my nerves. I asked them to take it again with a different blood pressure cuff. The nurse let me lay down for a few minutes with my feet up. She came back and used a different cuff. Nothing changed. The obstetrician, Dr. Anne, completed a cervical check. I was less than a centimeter dilated. It was hard to believe, since it felt like the baby had been ready to make her appearance for weeks now. She suggested I be induced within the next day, for the safety of me and the baby. I responded with,

"I won't do that because it's not how I planned it."

I'm surprised she didn't laugh at me. I think instead she mustered up all of her years of training on proper bedside manner and simply said, "Welcome to parenthood."

I sat, feet in stirrups, and refused to let my plans be interrupted. I was so angry. I had only prepared myself and educated myself on natural births. I refused to believe an induction would be part of my process. I didn't realize it then, but the Lord was beginning to allow *my* shiny, pristine "plan" to shatter. "For I know the plans I have for you, declares the Lord…" (Jeremiah 29:11a). I asked the doctor to complete a cervical membrane sweep as a last-ditch effort to jump-start labor. She did, and I bit my lip in pain.

• • •

Dr. Anne advised us to go home to talk through our options privately and let her know in the next few hours if I wanted to reserve my spot for an induction. As if I wanted to reserve a table at a popular restaurant.

Noah was quiet on that car ride home, which is unusual for him. He just let me cry and get snot everywhere, like any charming and well put-together wife. He was the epitome of gentleness. I can only imagine how he felt in that situation. I was a certified hot mess. He wore his work clothes to the appointment. We hadn't planned for this news. I assumed I would get another week of laying on the couch and waddling around the neighborhood. We had never planned for an induction. I told myself it wouldn't happen. I wanted to labor at home, where I could be comfortable. I only wanted to use the hospital when it was show time.

When we got home, Noah said that it was ultimately up to me, and he would support my decision either way. He said he was concerned about the high blood pressure. He wanted to keep the baby and me as safe as possible. I agreed, and he notified the doctor. I called my mentor from church, Megan, and we prayed together about it. Well, I cried and she did the praying.

"I'm scared I can't do it!" I told her. "Deliver a baby? And I don't know how to take care of a child, what am I thinking?"

"Lisa," she said, "If anyone can do it, you can! This is going to be amazing."

She believed in me when I felt helpless. She spoke truth when I felt only doubt. I need those kinds of people in my life.

Noah encouraged me to try to relax and eat since there was no guarantee I could eat during the labor. I tried to nap. I couldn't. I continued to fume about my "plan" unfurling. My mind was playing a questionnaire of fear on repeat.

What if the baby gets stuck and I need a C-section?
What if I made the wrong decision to get induced?
What if she has colic?
What if it hurts too much to breastfeed?
What if she's breech?
Will Noah still be attracted to me after this?
Will we be able to afford this?

And round and round it went.

I tried to explain the situation to Tulip. I knew it would be a hard transition for her. She was eight years old and had traveled with me all around the country when I worked on the road. We lavished her with all the affection and snuggles her bearded snout could handle, and I knew a baby would rock her world. More fear-filled questions:

Would she react badly?
Would she make angry poops under the baby's bed in a passive-aggressive way to let me know she's angry about the new addition?
Would she be devastated?

I cried and hugged her and gave her treats.

CHAPTER 3
Labor

At 7:55 p.m., I rode the elevator to the fourth floor of the hospital. It was a new hospital, and the style of the decor was an obvious mind trick to make me think I had arrived for a day at the spa. Calming music played in the hallways and soothing hues of lilac and gray were painted on the walls in soft brushstrokes. When a baby is born, the mother is pushed in a wheelchair with her new child to a wall painted blue with stars. The new mom pushes a button that lights up the stars and plays a lullaby. The whole hospital hears the lullaby so everyone in the building knows a baby has been born.

It hit me right in the hormones. I wanted to push that button.

After the nurse fumbled around in my left forearm with her IV needle for a while, the anesthesiologist was called. She stuck me in the right hand to administer electrolytes. I looked out the window to my right which showed a popular shopping area. For the customers in the stores, this was just another Thursday night. The doctor arrived, a mature and professional woman I had met during an office visit. The obstetrics department had six doctors on staff, all of whom could be on call when it came time for delivery. She completed a cervical check, and the area felt sore from the membrane sweep that morning. I was less than a centimeter dilated. The bun was cooked, but the oven door was shut.

The doctor stated she would administer Cervidil, which is a medication produced as a tampon-like vaginal insert. She suggested I try to relax and sleep while the medicine completed its twelve-hour process of thinning and softening the cervix. I received the medication at 10:30 p.m.

My body must not have listened to her instructions; it wanted to play a different game. The manufacturers of Cervidil note "contractions occurring at a faster rate than normal" is a common side effect of the medication that occurs in less than one out of twenty patients[2]. I should have bought a lottery ticket. The night nurse arrived to check on me within the hour after I was administered the medication.

"Oh, wow!" She told me with a big smile as she pointed to the waves on the monitor. "You're having some strong contractions! I've only had a couple other patients react this way. Most patients don't feel anything."

This did not seem to be good news for me, despite her enthusiasm.

She asked me how I felt, and I told her, "I'm fine. It's just pressure."

I labored with contractions every one to two minutes through the night. I couldn't understand what my body was doing. I had planned for my labor to begin at home. I wanted my water to break at home. I didn't want to be hooked up to belts and wires and IVs, but it was happening nonetheless. I understood the body's functions during natural births, but I knew nothing about medication and procedures used to induce labor. During pregnancy, I refused to acknowledge this as a possibility. I assumed the pain from synthetic chemicals forcing my body to contract and move in a manner it wasn't prepared for would be unbearable.

In this instance, I assumed correctly.

Noah slept on a padded bench the hospital provided which looked to be about the size of the baby bassinet. He didn't complain. I was awake. All night. Except for a half hour from 3:00 a.m. to 3:30 a.m. That's not even a decent nap. I watched the waves go up and down on the contraction monitor, growing higher and wider. I cried into my pillow in the dark to not wake Noah. I wanted him to be able to have as much energy as possible to help with the baby. In a combination of exhaustion and delusion, I stared at the tubes going to and from my body and thought, "O.K., it would be a little wild, but I can pull this IV out of my arm and sneak out past the nurse desk and go home. I'm not ready. I can't do it."

I hurt.

I prayed.

The Lord was silent.

* * *

7:00 a.m. is the shift change for the maternity ward. The doctor who initiated my induction was now being replaced by the same prim and poignant Dr. Anne who I had seen during my office visit less than twenty-four hours ago. She has a pretty face, the kind that would be painted on a porcelain doll. I was relieved to see her familiar smile, but then I saw her clothes. Blue scrubs.

Oh no.

Prior to today, I had only seen her in an office setting. She typically sported a tasteful business-casual skirt topped with a pressed blouse, little clicking heels and that clean white doctors coat. During those office visits, we had talked about the future and birth as if they were distant clouds that could never truly manifest into something tangible. Now, though, she was wearing blue scrubs and those shoes with heavy rubber soles to avoid slipping. *"Slipping in what?"* I thought. The scrubs meant this was serious. It meant that I am about to somehow get this miniature human out of my body and keep her alive.

"*I. Can't. Do. This.*" I thought. *"Is it too late to back out? Is it too late?"*

Dr. Anne explained that it was nearly time to remove the Cervidil and check my cervix for progress.

"Noah!" I shouted. He had dozed off between tosses and turns. He jumped up mid-snore with those *"Where-am-I-and-what-day-is-it?"* eyes.

"I need you! I need you! I need you!" I told him.

I pulled him down by the T-shirt and cried into his shoulder.

"I can't do this! I don't want to do this! I'm not going to make it!" I pleaded with him, "I can't have a baby, please make it stop! Please, please, please make it stop!"

I was hysterical. I was closing in on twenty-four hours with only a half-hour of sleep. My back seared with pain. Rational thought had left the building. The day-shift nurse, Brenda, entered our room. She has one of those personalities who creates a sense of trust and comfort, as if we had been friends for years and she also happened to be my nurse. It was clear she had found her calling and pursued it with sincerity.

It was time to remove the Cervidil insert. Dr. Anne began to reach for the insert and I cried and kicked her hand out of the way. This time the pain was excruciating. Dr. Anne stopped and explained that there was irritation to the skin surrounding the insert which had caused additional swelling to the vaginal wall. She explained to me that the medication can cause this type of reaction in some patients, which will make cervical checks extremely painful.

No kidding.

Dr. Anne applied some numbing cream to the area before she proceeded to remove the medicated insert. It took two nurses and Noah to hold me down long enough for Dr. Anne to remove the medication and check for progress without my legs involuntarily shoving her out of the way. The pain was unbearable. At approximately twelve hours into labor, she advised I was now one-and-one-half centimeters dilated, but my cervix had softened from the medication.

"That's all?! When is this going to be over?!" I continued in hysteria.

Dr. Anne told me that there was no way to know the time labor would end. I said, "You have to give me some idea of when this will end! Four hours? Six hours more? Eight more?"

She looked at me hesitantly and said, "There's no way to know for sure. It could be eight hours or it could take a couple of days."

I fell apart. I knew I was already tapped out emotionally and physically and I was only on the first lap of the race. At that point, Dr. Anne gave me some instructions that could be taken and applied to many difficult situations in life: "Take a shower. Eat. Close your eyes. I will come back in an hour, and we can discuss the next steps."

I was thankful for the shower, because I could cry as hard as I wanted and no one asked any questions. I felt like a failure. I knew I wouldn't make it to the end of labor the way I wanted. Did I make the wrong decision to be induced? Did I make the wrong decision to try and have a baby? My goal was to be without pain medicine, including an epidural. To tough it out. To be strong. To breathe deep. To listen to those guided meditation videos I had nearly memorized over the last half a year. To suck it up like a Samurai ninja and get the baby out by myself.

I didn't meet my goal. Self-condemnation rushed through me, although I knew this disappointment came from no one but myself. I knew I couldn't handle the pain of gloved hands shoving their way into my birth canal any longer. The contractions seemed to be perpetual and without respite. My body reacted to medication in its own unique way, and it made me furious. My pride began to be stripped away as I became vulnerable. I trusted in strangers in scrubs to make decisions for me and my unborn child.

After I dried off from the shower, I asked Noah to call his mom, Stephanie. Initially, I didn't want any family or friends in the delivery room until after the baby was born. I didn't want anyone other than Noah to see me in this state. Ironically, now that I was in such a state, I craved the presence of someone else who had been in my position and made it through to the other side. I needed someone to say, "I know. I've been there. It's going to be O.K." I knew Stephanie had been induced for all four of her children's births and I trusted her to understand this fear. Stephanie arrived at our room, but first she bought a stuffed bunny rabbit for the baby in the hospital gift shop. It was so soft, and it reminded me of the purpose in the pain.

My little daughter.

I asked Noah and Stephanie if I should get an epidural. They both told me there is no wrong way to deliver a baby. They also told me it was no one's choice but my own. I tried to roll on a birthing ball and leaned onto the bed to see if there was any tolerable position. I listened to music and tried to convince myself it was just pressure, not pain. Nothing helped to put the fire out in my body. I asked for an epidural. I asked for help.

The anesthesiologist arrived with a rolling cart of medical equipment. I was reminded of the risks associated with an epidural, as if I hadn't already demonized it sufficiently in my own mind. I consented. I was told to bend over in order to create room for the needle to access my spinal cord. The anesthesiologist was a clean-cut male who had either shaved or waxed off all of his arm hair. As he was sanitizing the area he asked, "Do you understand what is happening?"

"Yes," I replied.

"Do you know what I'm administering?" he asked.

"An epidural," I confirmed.

I was terrified. I began to cry uncontrollably and my sobs shook the bed. The anesthesiologist explained he couldn't proceed until I stopped moving. Noah held my right hand and nurse Brenda held the left until that "pop" of the needle pierced the threshold of my spine. Then the numbness took over. I was so relieved. I was able to finally rest as my legs were propped up in bed like entities which were now separate from my own body. I was given a catheter. I still couldn't fall asleep. Heartburn began to flood my throat. It was time for the next step in the induction process.

Dr. Anne explained she would insert a "balloon" into my cervix which would expand to quicken dilation. I was thankful to be numb. I hated the thought of how many hands and equipment had been in and out of an area that was clearly not yet ready to dilate for birth. The numerous cervical checks and procedures eliminated any sacred humanity from the experience of childbirth, despite the highest level of professionalism from Dr. Anne and nurse Brenda. This was a vulnerability I was not prepared for.

Noah and Stephanie each held one of my hands, and Dr. Anne inserted the balloon which would remain for several hours to open the cervix. After a few more hours, Stephanie packed up to leave us an opportunity to turn down the lights and rest. I was desperate for sleep, but my body was not willing to comply. After the balloon had completed its process, Dr. Anne removed the device and explained I was now four centimeters dilated.

It seemed like such a small improvement, although I was told that any progress is good progress. Dr. Anne said it was time to break my water.

I was thankful to be numb.

Dr. Anne planned to administer Pitocin later in the evening, a drug which forces longer and stronger contractions. I would begin with a low dose for a period of time, then the dosage would gradually increase. Dr. Anne suggested I eat a light meal for energy before the Pitocin began, which surprised me. I had anticipated not being able to eat anything other than those infamous hospital ice chips this far into the game. The food gave me physical energy, but it also increased my trust in Dr. Anne. She veered from procedure in response to my needs. She was on my team, and we both had the same goal.

Get the baby out.

I had a plain turkey sandwich and drank ginger ale for my heartburn. I was then encouraged, once again, to try and fall asleep.

* * *

7:00 p.m. was another shift change for the maternity ward. Except for Dr. Anne, the rest of the staff worked twelve-hour shifts. Nurse Brenda hugged me goodbye. She said she was disappointed not to have met my baby, but she assured me that soon enough I would be able to hold my child in my arms. The night nurse who replaced Brenda seemed to hate her job, and maybe hated me too. Most of her communication was one-syllable answers and sighs of irritation. I imagined she thought my difficulties were no different than the hundreds of others she had observed through the years and I wasn't unique.

Although the epidural helped to numb my lower half, my hips continued to throb in pain. I had heartburn so intense I could feel the acid sitting and brewing in my lower esophagus. Delirium was unavoidable as I had slept only thirty minutes in the last forty hours. The clock ticked-tocked into another night. At one point, I pulled off my blood pressure monitor that had been inflating and deflating every hour since I arrived at the hospital. Between the IV fluids that stuck in my hand, the contraction monitor which wrapped around my stomach, and the catheter I couldn't even feel, I was trapped and tied in by these clear tubes and beeping machines. The anesthesiologist gave me a button I could push every twenty minutes if I needed extra pain medication through the epidural. I pushed it hundreds of times, hoping I could trick the machine into being more generous. I considered asking for a C-section, but I was too afraid of the thought of surgery. I had no more desire to meet this baby, I just wanted to go home. Noah was able to doze off and on as he spent his second night on the sleep bench. Not a bed, just a bench. As I approached midnight of my second night of labor, I began to sob. I began to believe I wouldn't survive this ordeal. I truly wanted to be put out of my misery into death.

Although I had been praying to the Lord through this nightmare, I couldn't find a rock to hold onto. I had no control, that much was evident. I wanted to will my body into submission, but I couldn't. I couldn't even move my own legs without someone else's help. I prayed to the Lord to take me. I prayed for him to let me die. All my will was lost. Then, suddenly, He spoke into my soul. I had reached a hopelessness and desperation I didn't know was possible. I had no distractions. No pride. Nowhere to escape. Just like the basement in my in-law's house, I was in a position where I could do nothing but listen.

I learned two lessons.

I had become vain. The Lord revealed to me that I had developed a prideful attitude towards other women. I thought I was better than everyone else. Stronger. Healthier. More disciplined. In my mind I had belittled those who didn't pursue a natural birth and condemned them for exposing their unborn child to medications, interventions, or surgeries. *Look at me now.* Judgement towards others felt comfortable. I had somehow created a system for competition within pregnancy and childbirth — who could exhibit the most will power?

I learned that competition allows no room for compassion.

I was hit hard with the truth that my body is frail and temporary. It's not strong or weak, disciplined or lazy, attractive or repulsive. It's just a body. It was created to expire, but to first be a house for my soul during my time on earth. The Kingdom of God allows no room for my vanity. The Lord plucked me off my pedestal so I could see that my physical capabilities were never created to be a source of pride.

> "All go to one place. All are from the dust, and to dust all return."
>
> Ecclesiastes 3:20 (ESV)

The second lesson I learned was where to keep my focus during times of struggle. I needed to look in the eyes of Jesus. I was far from home, the darkness of this night seemed endless, and I could see nothing but the storm.

> "Meanwhile, the disciples were in trouble far away from land, for a strong wind had risen, and they were fighting heavy waves. About three o'clock in the morning Jesus came toward them, walking on the water. When the disciples saw him walking on the water, they were terrified. In their fear, they cried out, "It's a ghost!"

> But Jesus spoke to them at once. "Don't be afraid," he said. "Take courage. I am here!"
> Then Peter called to him, "Lord, if it's really you, tell me to come to you, walking on the water."
> "Yes, come," Jesus said.
> So, Peter went over the side of the boat and walked on the water toward Jesus. But when he saw the strong wind and the waves, he was terrified and began to sink. "Save me, Lord!" he shouted.
> Jesus immediately reached out and grabbed him. "You have so little faith," Jesus said. "Why did you doubt me?"
>
> Matthew 14: 24-31 (NLT)

I signed a waiver around 2:00 a.m. on my second day of labor which allowed the anesthesiologist to administer an opioid medication which would force my body to sleep for thirty minutes. This occurred after I begged the night nurse repeatedly for anything that would knock me out for some amount of sleep before it was time to push. I would have taken a blow to the head if that's what I needed to pass out for one moment of reprieve and rest from this desperate misery. I couldn't see straight after two days without sleep, and I certainly couldn't think straight. Like those screeching canaries that peck and claw at their cages in a pet store, I just wanted out.

I fell into a graciously unconscious state for exactly thirty minutes, until the alarms started to wail. One of the IV bags was empty of fluids, and the machine was angry about it. Me too. I called the nurse's station, and I was advised a nurse would soon arrive to switch the bags. It beeped and beeped and beeped for nearly ten minutes until Noah walked to the nurse's station himself, and didn't leave until someone came back with him to turn off the foghorn. I told the night nurse that my hips were on fire with pain, and she said she would check the progress of my dilation.

"Yep, that's why it hurts," she told me. "Baby's ready."

• • •

Dr. Anne was called, and I caught a final wind of energy. The wait was over. Blue scrubs began to file in my room, each stood with gloves on. They were ready to pounce. At thirty hours into labor, it was time to push that bowling ball out. I learned to watch the contraction monitor and force my body to rest as the waves went downward, then it was time to push as I approached the peak of each wave. After fifteen minutes of pushing, some of the nurses began to look at each other and whisper a message I wasn't allowed to hear. They didn't look happy. Finally, Dr. Anne spoke up and let me know that everything was going to be fine. However, the baby's face was turned downward and she seemed to be stuck. Typically, the baby is positioned with her face to the front of the mother's abdomen in order for the spinal column to stay in a neutral bend as it travels through the birth canal.

Not my baby; she had to do things differently.

Dr. Anne kept an atmosphere of calm in the room as she explained this position didn't make a vaginal birth impossible, but was simply more difficult and a lengthy process. Instead of pushing as I had been, she instructed the night nurse to hold one end of a towel and I would hold the other. When a contraction came, I would focus on pulling the towel into my body as she pulled back instead of pushing my abdomen down into my hips. This would alter the angle of pressure to compensate for the change in the baby's head position.

I couldn't do it. Not by myself. The waves were too strong. The towel tug of war began, and I closed my eyes each time a contraction came. I closed my eyes to see the body of Jesus who stood in full confidence amidst the storm, holding onto my hand even then. Never letting go. He was bright enough to illuminate the darkness. When my eyes were open my head fell into Noah's arms and my body shook from exhaustion. Noah wiped the sweat off of my forehead. I was burning up. My mouth was dry. It was hard to swallow and impossible to take a full breath. Each contraction I would tell myself, *"Lisa, this is the last one,"* and then close my eyes.

"One more time," my eyes shut.

"Last one," Jesus' hand in mine.

"This is it," the light shines in the darkness.

After an hour, it was over. The relief was inexplicable. Lorelai Marie made quite an entrance. She was placed on my chest within seconds, and then she got a cute hat. I looked down and saw a perfect baby. A nurse removed the mucus from her nose, the fluid in her throat, and she cried. Me too. I spoke to her because I trusted she would find comfort in the familiarity of my voice.

"That was really hard, wasn't it?" I asked her. "But you did it! I'm so proud of you!"

Noah wept with his whole body. She wrapped her hand around his pinky, as if she had been waiting nine months to do just that – to hold her daddy's hand.

CHAPTER 4
The First Week

I was so thankful to be done with labor and to not be pregnant anymore. Dr. Anne stitched a first-degree tear, and then the epidural was removed and sensation returned to my legs. I tried to eat, but I was nauseated. My legs shook. Noah held Lorelai as the delivery room was cleared out and I was transferred in a wheelchair to a different hospital room. My postpartum nurse's name was Fran, and she said she had worked in a maternity ward for thirty-eight years. It showed. She was calm and efficient. Fran suggested Lorelai have as much skin-to-skin time as possible, so Noah tucked his baby into the center of his chest and covered her back with a fleece blanket. He said it was the happiest moment of his life and I believed him.

. . .

It was not my happiest moment. My legs and abdomen would not stop shaking as the adrenaline pulsed through my body. Everything hurt. I was afraid to get up to go to use the restroom for the first time. I thought Lorelai looked like a beautiful baby, but I had no desire to hold her. I was just tired. I was wondering when the instant connection between Lorelai and me would happen. Other mothers described their first moments with their child as an experience of falling in love. I just wanted to go home. I wanted to eat and sleep and take a shower and pet the dog. I wanted to be left alone.

Smile and nod, smile and nod. Everything is fine.

I was told these were the magical moments that I needed to savor and enjoy. I expected my life to be automatically fuller and sweeter as soon as I became a mother. That is what all the greeting cards from my baby shower told me to expect. I was *supposed* to enjoy every single moment. This was *supposed* to be the moment I fell in love with my baby.

Why did this moment hurt so bad?

The lactation consultant arrived. Her hair was long and blonde and she was in full makeup to boot. I asked her if she had children.

"Six," she said.

Six? *Children?* My mind could not comprehend having six of these.

"You are going to be so amazed to see what you can do with only a few hours of sleep," she told me. "Women are incredible."

She said I looked exhausted. I said "Doesn't everybody look exhausted here?"

She stared me down and searched my face, then replied, "Yes. But you look *really* exhausted."

Was this an insult or just an observation? Regardless, she deemed me too exhausted to try to breastfeed for the first time. Lorelai was fast asleep on Noah's chest, and she explained I should try to do the same. She told nurse Fran that I should not be disturbed for an hour and a half to get some peace and quiet. I loved this lady with her luscious lipstick and brood of children. She explained that a ninety-minute nap could turn me into a new woman, and I believed her.

Once again, I could not sleep. After ninety minutes of staring at the ceiling, Lorelai began to stir, and the lactation consultant returned. She showed Noah how to give his baby a sponge bath, and how to change her diaper. She found him to be a very enthusiastic student. Then, it was time to breastfeed. I was afraid of breastfeeding, based on all that I had read and heard from friends. I was told it would be painful, and it may take a while for Lorelai or me to have success. I read that newborn babies often nursed 8-12 times per day in the early weeks, and I assumed this would become my part-time job. I had set low expectations for this part.

Trying to hold Lorelai in a position to nurse was awkward. I was afraid I was going to drop her or make her uncomfortable. I will credit Lorelai for being smart enough to figure out nursing despite my own fumbling. Once a latch was established, the lactation consultant seemed to be happy with Lorelai's sounds and movements that I observed for the first time. It was not painful, but it was not comfortable either. Uterine contractions began and stole my breath with pain once the nursing started, but the consultant explained to me that contractions were a good sign that my body was responding to Lorelai.

I thought the contractions were over, but no.

Then the family started to come visit. I was happy for them to meet Lorelai and ogle and coo over her, but all I wanted was to go home. I wanted to be home by myself in my own bed. It's all I could think about. Stephanie had worked as a nurse for decades so I asked her to help me to the bathroom for the first time since birth. My legs shook with weakness as she held my elbow and led me to the bathroom. She helped to gently lower me down onto the toilet, and the pain was excruciating. I had no bladder control. I had expected a substantial amount of blood within the first forty-eight hours after giving birth, but it still shocked me. I cried. Stephanie said the only thing I needed to hear:

"I know it hurts. I've been there. I get it."

Then I learned how to use that squirt water bottle. Lord have mercy. Stephanie applied the numbing spray to my body. It was a moment of humility. Then she poured the cooling green goop onto the fluffy pillow of a sanitary pad which then went into the underwear. Giant mesh underwear. Stephanie led me back to my bed where I continued to shake as if my hand was stuck on an electric fence.

Lorelai cried, as babies do. She slept, as babies do. I fed her every three hours, and she had ample dirty diapers. Now that the labor was over, it seemed like everything was looking up. Those honeymoon hormones were pumping, and nurse Fran told me I was doing well with breastfeeding. Night approached, as did another 7:00 p.m. shift change. Nurse Fran told me she would be back tomorrow morning, and she was replaced by a younger night nurse with a long brown ponytail and beautiful olive skin. When it was time to feed, she positioned and repositioned Lorelai and myself until we both got in a good flow. She was aggressive and shoved Lorelai onto the target with force. It worked. I asked her to take Lorelai to the nursery until she needed to eat again, so I could try to sleep. She said that the hospital doesn't have a nursery anymore, but it was a slow night so she could watch Lorelai at her station. It seemed odd, but I just wanted to be left alone. I managed to doze in and out of a light slumber until Lorelai was returned in exactly three hours. Then again. And once more. Then nurse Fran returned at 7:00 a.m. It was Sunday.

Noah woke up like a child on Christmas when he saw Lorelai. He couldn't wait to hold her. I didn't want to. I just wanted to nurse her the recommended number of minutes, and then put her in someone else's arms so that I could rest. My legs continued to shake, but not as violently. The pain from birth was intense, but I was given NSAIDs to help. Stephanie brought a bouquet of pink tulips, and my mom had a small azalea shrub delivered with fresh spring blooms. I asked nurse Fran if I would be able to go home on that Sunday, and she said I was not ready yet. I knew I was not ready, but I wanted to be out of the hospital. Noah loved to let Lorelai rest on his chest for skin-to-skin time, and I loved to watch. He was giddy, and she was in bliss.

We continued to learn about how to keep a newborn alive, and we survived another day of feeding, burping, diaper changing, and holding. I knew objectively that Lorelai was an excellent baby. Healthy. Strong. Sleeping easily. Yet, she was a stranger. A stranger that I didn't have any desire to get to know. Someone unpredictable who spoke a language I couldn't decipher. I smiled and nodded and said what people wanted to hear.

"Yes, it is difficult, but she is so worth it!"

"I'm so in love with her!"

"I can't wait to bring her home!"

I thought if I said it enough to other people, I would begin to believe it myself.

On Monday morning, I was allowed to leave after five days in the hospital.

* * *

Nurse Fran wheeled me down to the hospital lobby. Noah ran outside to pull the car up. There was snow. I sat in a wheelchair. *Somehow they think I'm strong enough to raise a child, but not strong enough to walk down the hall.*

I saw the hospital gift shop to my left which sold products that now seemed meaningless. The hospital doors opened to my right and the sun came through the snow, making everything shine. *This is good.* I saw Lorelai, and I knew I loved her. I didn't feel it, but I already had come to admire her for the intrinsic character traits I saw she possessed.

Kindness.

Gentleness.

Bravery.

Happy tears finally formed, and I told nurse Fran, "I can't believe I get to bring her home. She's perfect, isn't she?"

She said, "Lisa, this is a special moment."

I nodded because I knew she was right.

She said, "Lisa, you will be a wonderful mom."

I nodded and I hoped she was right.

She hugged me as I cried, and then Noah pulled up the car to take us home.

• • •

On our way home we got Chick-fil-A sandwiches with extra pickles. We laughed about how funny Lorelai looked in the unicorn outfit we chose for her homecoming. We kept giving each other that look of "*can you believe this is happening? This is the moment. This is the time we've been waiting for.*"

Noah carried Lorelai up the stairs, and the first thing he did was give her a tour of our apartment. "This is where you will sleep. This is where Mommy and Daddy sleep. This is where we will give you your first bath. This is your home now too, Lorelai."

That evening, my in-laws came over to bring dinner. Roast chicken with vegetables and a crunchy baguette. It was good.

Then we realized Lorelai's Pack-n-Play wouldn't fit in the space we had planned to use, and I got so upset. Noah and his stepdad had to move furniture around, and it felt overwhelming to me. Suddenly our space seemed too small and the challenge seemed too big. Too many changes, too much newness. I started to cry and Stephanie came over and hugged me. She looked me in the eyes with the same look I had seen before: *I've been there. I've felt what you are feeling.*

She said, "Lisa, it's O.K. to cry."
So, I did.
She said, "Lisa, this is what family is for."

* * *

After Stephanie and Dan left, Lorelai began to cry. And she didn't stop. I knew this moment would come, the moment where Noah and I were left alone to try and "figure it out." We checked the possible culprits: Hungry? Nope, just ate. Dirty? Wet? Nope, clean diaper. Gassy? No. She was just being a baby. I made sure there wasn't a volume button on her that I had missed. Maybe they took it with the umbilical cord? We swaddled her, offered a pacifier, walked with her, talked with her, rhythmically shushed her, and nothing stopped her cries. She continued for thirty minutes, and I couldn't believe she hadn't passed out yet from the sobs. I offered her the option to nurse again, which she rejected.

I held her tight with her head on my shoulder and her stomach against my chest. I rocked in the rocking chair and sang "Jesus Loves Me." It didn't make her stop crying, but it helped to calm me. I kept singing and rocking for myself, and the effect eventually worked on Lorelai. She calmed down enough to nurse again. Then she fell asleep. Just like a baby does. The cycle of sleep, eat, poop, sleep, eat, poop was an easy concept to grasp, but somehow it seemed so complicated. I had a college degree; I was able to think big thoughts at one point.

She slept two hours until her next cries to nurse. I had planned to be the only parent up during the night with Lorelai, since I was the one with the breastfeeding equipment. I didn't want to have Noah deprived of sleep as well. I figured one of us had to keep our wits about us. When she cried, I picked her up, changed her diaper, nursed her, burped her, wrapped her in the swaddle from the hospital, and swayed back and forth with her in my arms. She slept in the top part of the Pack-n-Play, on her back, and her head turned to the right. It was clearly the direction her head had been positioned in the womb, and she wasn't interested in changing it. The Pack-n-Play was in our bedroom, and I could hear every twitch and sniffle our new little creature made.

Mom ears. It's a real thing.

Nursing with Lorelai seemed to be going well, based on her ample pees and poops and deep sleeps. I had pain in nursing, since we were both learning how to use the built-in milk machinery for the first time. That first night at home, I slept an hour and then another hour before the sun came up. I couldn't relax. I kept looking at the clock. My back spasmed and my legs shook. Pain resulting from the delivery remained intense. I ate and chugged water through the night hours, but sleep was elusive. The following morning, I fixed breakfast to try and feel "normal." Toast. Peanut butter. Familiar comforts from my old life.

Then I took a shower. It humbled me. My knees wobbled. I couldn't control my bladder. I couldn't see straight. I looked down and realized most of my left forearm was bruised from the IV. I was amazed at the amount of red that stood against the white tile. I didn't realize my body could hurt so fiercely. I decided then that regardless of how much sleep I was able to get, I would do my best to shower every day, to brush my hair, and to smell like something other than hot spit up. It made a world of difference. A shower was a metamorphosis from life in zombie-mode to life in color as a functioning human being.

It was Tuesday, and Noah had the rest of the work week to be at home. He looked tired, yet enamored with his daughter and life in general. Tulip had been up all night with me, pacing from the bedroom to the living room and back. She didn't know what to think. She couldn't understand why we were making such a big deal over this loud, naked puppy who couldn't seem to do anything for herself. She watched as Noah held Lorelai on his chest, petting her peach-fuzz head and playing with her fingers. She had long fingers and toes, which Noah decided would be very good at strumming guitar.

I had planned to sleep when the baby sleeps, but this turned out to be difficult. Lorelai slept like a champion, but I began to have visions of the hospital delivery room when I tried to close my eyes. I tried to relax, but my body wouldn't be still. Shockwaves flowed to every part of my body. I put on music to distract myself, but my mind continued to return to the scenes from the hospital. The most painful memories of the birth flooded back in my mind *over* and *over* and *over* again. I couldn't stop myself from reliving it.

The pain.

The fear.

The darkness.

I found myself doing things like the laundry and the dishes instead of being able to lay down. I had to do them secretly, without Noah seeing me. He would be upset if he saw me doing anything other than resting, but it felt comfortable to do chores that I had completed thousands of times before. I knew the motions, and I could breathe easier with everything in order. Noah loved to sit and hold Lorelai when she was asleep and talk to her when she was awake. He watched golf, drank coffee, and kept her forehead covered in sweet kisses. I liked to look at her, but I didn't want to hold her.

She was the most beautiful baby I had ever seen. She had dark, wavy hair like Noah. Her eyes were newborn grey and mostly closed. Because of her posterior position during labor, the ridges between the plates of her skull were more pronounced due to the extra pressure. The deep ridges made me proud of her because they signified her survival through a tough journey. She had already been through quite a lot during her first few days outside of the womb.

On Wednesday, my parents came to Ohio to see us and meet Lorelai. I slept four hours the prior night, and I felt better. Four hours was twice as many as two, so I was encouraged by the upswing. The honeymoon hormones were surging, and friends were dropping in to bring hot meals and cute clothes for our new addition. The intensity of the pain from birth had decreased as my body was hurriedly putting things back in place after the wreckage. We watched baking shows on television, and I wiped down the kitchen counter repeatedly.

On Thursday, I turned thirty years old. *Happy birthday, Mommy.* I showered and put on makeup and soft pajamas. I had slept another four hours the night before, and Lorelai continued to excel at nursing and sleeping. I cried alone a few times, both happy and sad tears. Naps were still out of the question as the scenes from the hospital were on repeat in my mind's eye. My mom did the dishes and the laundry for me, but I still found items to clean and organize. I couldn't help myself. Two separate people arrived with a birthday cake, and I had a slice of each. One was a red velvet Bundt cake with cream cheese icing, and the other one was classic white with buttercream and, "Happy Birthday, Lisa" written in cursive yellow frosting. I couldn't pick a favorite. That night I started to have pain in my lower back, but I thought nothing of it.

On Friday, we took Lorelai to her pediatric appointment, and she was back to her birth weight. I had to fill out the Edinburgh Postnatal Depression Scale for the second time. I was still determined to not experience postpartum depression. Other than the emotional swings which are part of sleep deprivation, I felt stable. I completed the questionnaire without any points awarded for postpartum depression, so the appointment was a win for me and a win for Lorelai. *This is good.*

My lower back began to hurt more and more, but I assumed it was some part of the recovery process. I had a lot of things to think about, and my sore back wasn't one of them. I took acetaminophen. My parents drove back to Tennessee, and I began to feel weak by the evening. I was short-tempered with Noah. Lorelai slept regular three-hour stretches, but my supernatural new-mom energy that surged earlier in the week had begun to diminish.

By evening on Friday, I noticed a sharp pain in my lower back that crept into my abdomen. *"It's just part of the process,"* I continued to tell myself. *"It's just cramps."* Each time I woke that night to nurse Lorelai I checked the thermostat. It was set at the normal temperature, but I was freezing. *"Must be broken,"* I thought. I sweat through my clothes, but shivered from chills. My teeth chattered. Hot then cold then hot then cold. I nursed Lorelai. I had to take care of her. I had to ignore any pain.

Saturday morning, I looked at the clock. 6:14 a.m. It was March 24th, and Lorelai was one week old. *Happy Birthday, Baby.* I took my temperature. The numbers kept growing. Then finally four loud beeps and a blinking red light. 103.9 degrees.

CHAPTER 5
Sick

"Something's wrong. Can you help me?" I whispered to Noah. He was still asleep. It was early. I told him I had a fever.

In a moment of brilliance, I assured him, "Don't worry! I'm sure it's no big deal! I'll just wait until the walk-in clinic opens and they can order me an antibiotic. No big deal. Maybe it's a bladder infection. I've heard of people getting bladder infections after they give birth."

I truly believed that a walk-in clinic was an appropriate option for me. I also hadn't slept enough to put together logical streams of thought. Noah explained I needed to call the hospital instead, that a walk-in clinic was not the best resource for a woman who just gave birth last weekend. I explained I didn't want to contact the hospital because I just left that place. That place is where my nightmares came to life. He dialed the number anyway and put the call on speaker. We got through to the doctor on call and explained the status. She told us to come into the hospital right away.

"Go to the fourth floor, Labor and Delivery," she said.

I told her I couldn't do that. I explained I had just left the fourth floor and I was not interested in a return. Not an option. I couldn't go back to that place again. She repeated her command to come to the hospital immediately, and she seemed flabbergasted that we were still having this discussion.

Noah told me, "It's going to be fine. Just take a shower. Don't worry about anything else. Just take a shower and put on your coat."

He threw clothes and diapers in Lorelai's bag and put Tulip into her crate. I showered and I put on my coat. We drove through a snowy sunrise to get to the hospital. I hate the snow. We had come back to the place that scared me the most. It was surreal. I was bent over in pain, but I didn't want anyone to see. I checked in and was led to a triage room.

"I just have a fever and my back hurts," I explained to the nurse. "But it's not so bad. I'm O.K., I just need some rest. Maybe I'm just tired."

She took a cornucopia of bodily fluids to test. She gave me ibuprofen for the fever and pain. I was given IV electrolytes. She saw I was upset. She said she was the head nurse of the unit for the day, and I was her special patient. She promised to be attentive. She held my hand while she told me all of this, and maintained eye contact until I believed her. I could see she meant it. I cried. She said it was good for me to cry right now, because there was a lot of change going on in my body. I drank ice water and shivered. She explained she was also a mom. Her son recently turned two years old, and she was ready to have another baby. She told me that she had worked in a labor and delivery unit for years before becoming pregnant herself. She told me she thought it would be an easier transition to motherhood, since she handled hundreds of newborns. It wasn't easier.

"Nothing can prepare you to become a mom," she told me. "There's nothing else like it."

She had thick glasses with purple rims, and her eyeshadow sparkled. She brought three warm blankets into the triage room. She gave one to Noah who sat in a chair to my left. She laid one over me, and swaddled Lorelai with the third blanket. She nestled the baby into her car seat like a warm burrito. She turned off the lights and laid my bed flat. She said I needed to try to sleep.

I closed my eyes. The on-call doctor was one of six in the practice, but I had never met her before. We waited for her to review the lab results. I anticipated the doctor would announce this was a run-of-the-mill bladder infection, perhaps a result of the catheter during birth. I would be ordered a prescription antibiotic and be able to get home before lunch time. Sleep evaded me once again, but my Spirit reminded me of a song I learned as a child in elementary school. I hadn't thought about this song in years, but I repeated it in my mind to keep my thoughts occupied until I heard more information from the doctor. I listened to the ancient words of the shepherd king:

> "The Lord is my shepherd,
> I shall not want.
> He makes me lie down in green pastures;
> He leads me beside quiet waters.
> He restores my soul;
> He guides me in the paths of righteousness
> For His name's sake.
> Even though I walk through the valley of the shadow of death,
> I fear no evil, for You are with me;
> Your rod and Your staff, they comfort me.
> You prepare a table before me in the presence of my enemies;
> You have anointed my head with oil;
> My cup overflows.
> Surely goodness and lovingkindness will follow me all the days of my life.
> I will dwell in the house of the Lord forever."
> Psalm 23, of David (NASB).

The doctor came in. *More blue scrubs.* She asked me about my symptoms, and checked my temperature. The ibuprofen worked and the fever had lowered to 101 degrees and I was "soaked" with sweat, as she put it. I saw this as a good sign that I would be able to leave soon. She typed notes into her computer and said she would return quickly with the lab results. After several minutes she returned with the nurse. The lights were still dimmed, and Lorelai slept soundly. The doctor sat down in her rolling chair next to my bed and she didn't look happy.

She explained that my lab results showed a high white blood cell count. An infection had set in. She explained that my symptoms and labs indicated a uterine infection, which is not uncommon after giving birth. However, most uterine infections set in quickly while the mother is still at the hospital after delivering a baby. She explained that for my situation, the induction and lengthy labor had kept my cervix open for an extended period of time which allowed opportunities for bacteria to enter the uterus. She hypothesized that the infection had been "brewing" all week, multiplying, and growing to become a major threat to my body.

This was serious.

She suggested I be admitted to the hospital for IV antibiotics, and to remain under observation until I was without a fever for twenty-four hours. I reacted in tears, and I raised my voice in anger towards her, "I have to go *HOME!* Please let me go home, please! I need to see my dog! I need to be in my bed! I need to be *home;* I just had a baby! Why can't you understand that?"

The doctor looked to the nurse and Noah, who both kept a hesitant silence. I begged her for an alternative, anything that would let me leave. I was given two other options. The first was to remain for a single dose of IV antibiotics, then return to the medical practice every day for thirty days to receive a

Clindamycin shot. She said the shots hurt, it would be difficult to maintain a daily appointment with a newborn in tow, and it may have adverse effects on breastmilk. Her second alternative was to complete a single dose of IV antibiotics, then prescribe a high dose of the oral antibiotic Augmentin for thirty days. However, when I had been prescribed Augmentin as a child, I experienced violent side effects of vomiting, diarrhea, and extreme nausea. Additionally, the doctor advised that the drug may also have an adverse effect on breastmilk. In short, if I wanted to keep breastfeeding, I had to stay put in the hospital for a while.

My head fell back into the bed, too tired to keep crying. My body sweat and shivered as it continued to fight against this illness that I didn't want to acknowledge. My mind felt like it had been pushed too far past the breaking point. It was then that I checked out. Numb. I couldn't withstand the challenges anymore, and I surrendered. I gave up fighting or feeling. Being numb was the only way to survive that situation. I stopped thinking about Lorelai, or Noah, or myself. I turned my face away from the doctor and the beeping monitors and the bag of fluid that dripped down into a tube into a vein into an arm that led to a body which I no longer felt was my own. I let the darkness envelope me. The doctor and nurse spoke to each other, then to me, but I couldn't understand them. It was like hearing voices underwater.

Noah had to make decisions for me. I wasn't capable anymore. His parents came. They talked in whispers. They made decisions. I could only stare at the ceiling. Someone wheeled me down to a hospital room at the end of the hall. I refused to eat or drink. I refused to be comforted or told, "It's going to be O.K." I only stared straight ahead and let my mind leave the hospital and go to a safer place. Lorelai stayed with us in the hospital room.

I was given my first bag of antibiotics and fell asleep for thirty minutes. I nursed Lorelai, and once again I felt trapped with the clear tubes and cords that wrapped around my arms.

My fever broke after six hours, and I was instructed I would be allowed to leave if the temperature stayed down for the next twenty-four hours. The head nurse with the purple glasses lived out her promise to me. She was attentive and came to my room when she had a break from other patients. She continued to offer me food and drink until I obliged and nibbled on crackers. She said her goal was to get me home as soon as possible. Later, the night nurse came in for her shift, and she smelled like waffles with maple syrup. She brought me a whole cake, the ones that new moms get as a congratulations for birthing a child. She said I deserved an extra one. I stuck a plastic fork into the center of the pink fondant and took a bite. It was dry.

I slept a couple hours that night, between Lorelai's feedings. I felt better on Sunday, and the fever stayed at bay. I ate breakfast and walked down the hall, no longer bent over in pain. It was nice. Noah's parents brought us lunch. Lorelai slept and ate and cried, as babies do. Noah held her while she was asleep and also while she was awake. As long as he was awake, he wanted to hold his daughter. She gave him a smile. He kissed her forehead.

I finished five bags of broad-spectrum antibiotics. We were released to go home Sunday afternoon at 4:00 p.m. I had the same nurse with the purple glasses, and she wheeled me out of the hospital room. I realized I never had the opportunity to press the button on the blue wall of stars when Lorelai was born. I had forgotten. I asked the nurse if it was too late to press the button, and she said she would be honored to wheel me to the twinkling wall. I pushed the big black button and watched the stars shine.

The lullaby rang through the hallways, and the nurses clapped for me. Now, I could leave.

We stopped by a drugstore on the way home, and Noah bought me acetaminophen and ibuprofen. I was released with the recommendation to take one of these two medications for pain every four hours, and to monitor my condition closely. I was instructed to seek immediate care if I noticed an increase in temperature or pain levels. I was still in pain, but it had considerably improved from last week. The human body is resilient. We gave Lorelai a bath and she hated it. I took a shower and I loved it. I embraced the capabilities of the twenty-first century and sent a grocery order to be picked up the following day. Monday. The day Noah returned to work.

• • •

Monday morning arrived, as it seems to do quite often. My pain levels were tolerable with acetaminophen and ibuprofen. I ate, but I had no appetite. I was nervous. Noah left, and the door closed behind him. He was sad to go, to leave "his girls." He locked the deadbolt into place with a click. I placed Lorelai in her rocker, and she fell asleep. I put on music, then I turned it off. I put on the T.V., but then I turned it off. I started a load of laundry. There was more of it now. Tulip's deep brown eyes looked as tired as mine. I gave her some snuggles and offered her Mr. Owl, her favorite toy that had somehow withstood many terrier thrashings over the years. She wasn't interested. She seemed sad and confused about what to do with this tiny creature. Me too, pup. Me too.

I cried constantly. As did Lorelai.

That afternoon, after several failed attempts and awkward jabs, I was able to wrangle her into the car by myself. I drove half a block down the road to fill up my car with gas, and she cried the entire trip. I checked on her after I parked, and I saw she had dumped chunky spit up down her neck. Gross. I wiped her down and changed her shirt, which only seemed to make her cry louder. I drove to the grocery store to pick up an order I had requested to be brought out to my car.

Lorelai continued to wail her sad little song as we drove to and from the grocery store. When I arrived back at our apartment, I realized the error in my ways. The groceries were in the trunk but who would carry them up the three flights of stairs? I looked at Lorelai who had spit up again. Again? I knew I couldn't leave her to carry my groceries. Instead of phoning a friend or just leaving them in the car until later, I thought it would be a good idea to do it myself. I detached her car seat and secured it on my right arm. I put a bag of frozen groceries in my left hand, and I started to walk towards the door. The weather was windy and cold, which matched my mood. Two school-aged boys paused their soccer game nearby to stare at the crazy lady. I walked gingerly because I knew I carried too much weight for a woman who just gave birth. However, because I just gave birth, I could not seem to think rationally enough to find a better solution. I carried the crying baby and a bag of groceries up the stairs, and I stopped at each landing to catch my breath. I did this twice more, and then left the rest in the trunk.

That first day alone, I couldn't seem to do anything to console Lorelai when she was upset. I couldn't find a way to hold her that she liked. She didn't want a pacifier. She ate plenty and had the diapers to prove it. I cried. I turned on the television, but the volume seemed to motivate her to be louder. I played music, but she didn't care. Once she fell asleep, she was very cute. Although unpredictable. She made me nervous. Anything could happen! I didn't want to be around her. I wanted her to go away while I slept for days. Or years.

After many lifetimes, Noah came home from work. People told me the days would be long, and they were right. Lorelai had a difficult time in the evening. As babies do. She cried. And cried some more. It was amazing how much volume could erupt from that tiny pink mouth. Noah was the only one able to calm her down in the evenings. He held her face-to-face. One hand held her head, and the other hand supported her body. He sang to her in his deepest voice, picking song after song until one of them did the trick. "L-O-V-E" by Nat King Cole was the ticket. She would stare at him wide eyed and open-mouthed in surprise. By the time Noah had spelled L-O-V-E three times, she would quiet down. That night she slept in solid three-hour increments, as did I. It was the best night of sleep yet.

On Tuesday, at ten days postpartum, I became sick.

I began having diarrhea every hour. Nursing Lorelai became a challenge. I often stopped mid-feed, put her back into her bed, and ran to the bathroom. I could hear her screaming. She was justifiably angry for being cut off quickly and left by herself. What was going on with my body? I was alarmed, but I assumed this stomach upset would end quickly. I drank water and ate bananas and yogurt. I had experienced these symptoms of stomach upset in the past during periods of high stress. My bowels get nervous when I get nervous.

Noah calls it "a case of the doo-doo squeals."

I was too afraid to take an anti-diarrheal medication while nursing. What if it hurt Lorelai's stomach? I was also too afraid to call my doctor and tell them of these symptoms. What if they asked me to go back to the hospital? The emergency room? I was too afraid to do anything but stay home and wait for this to end. I was embarrassed. If I were to leave with Lorelai, what if I had to use the bathroom while driving? I did some laundry and cleaned the kitchen. I called Noah to tell him I seemed to have some sort of a stomach bug. He asked what he could do to help. I told him I didn't know.

After a day and night of this bout with my bowels, I noticed a significant weight loss. I called the obstetrics practice to schedule a follow-up appointment from my hospitalization the past weekend. I was exhausted, and Lorelai was a ball of needs. I grew resentful. She had emptied me, and only demanded more. More energy. More time. More comfort. More laundry. More diapers. Her needs seemed endless, but my body couldn't keep up. I convinced myself that the diarrhea was associated with this panic-stricken state of mind I had developed. I told myself if I could just calm down, my bowels would then calm down, and everything would be fine.

I was not calm.

I had visions of myself throwing Lorelai through our glass doors and over the balcony. Then she would be quiet. Then this would be over. My own thoughts terrified me, and I decided to not tell Noah about them. Or anyone else for that matter. I assumed someone would have to come take the baby away if I confessed these thoughts. I imagined a uniformed officer arriving at our apartment to label me unfit to parent and then send me off to a psychiatric ward. I considered dropping her off anonymously at a fire station and driving away across the country until I melted into silent obscurity. I wondered what my family would think if I gave her to the state.

I cried continually and my body began to shake once again, as if my hand returned to the live wire on the electric fence. *What if I stopped producing milk from this diarrhea? What if they make me go back to the hospital? What if I have to get more antibiotics? What if this doesn't stop? What if I can't sleep again tonight?*

What if I can never sleep again? What if Lorelai can't sleep tonight? What if she gets sick? What if she loses weight? What if we can't afford the hospital bills when they are due? What if I am a terrible mother for not wanting to be around her?

All thoughts became extremes.

In the chaos, I was reminded by the Spirit of God of His word in Philippians 4:13, "I can do all things through Christ who strengthens me."

I said it out loud.

"I can do all things through Christ who strengthens me."

And again.

"I can do all things through Christ who strengthens me."

And again. And again. And again. Until I began to believe the words for myself.

Noah came home from work, and we tried to stuff food into our mouths and called it dinner. I downed more kefir and toast. I was angry that I didn't get to be with my husband alone. I missed him. He missed me. Lorelai cried. I cried. I felt guilty that Noah had to come home to a crying baby and a crying wife. I didn't know what to do. I slept some, but my mind began to race faster and faster as each hour passed. I couldn't take a deep breath. My stomach continued to demand my time through the night. It felt like a nightmare. Everything hurt.

Is this how it feels to be a mom?

* * *

When I stepped on the scale at the doctor's office the following afternoon, I was three pounds below my pre-pregnancy weight. I was twelve days postpartum. My hands shook. The nurse commented that breastfeeding can cause rapid weight loss. I had Lorelai with me in her stroller, and she cried. We had sat in the waiting room for twenty minutes, which she decided was too long for her. It was raining outside. I completed the Edinburgh Postnatal Depression Scale questionnaire for the third time since giving birth. My answers were different now.

Everything was different now.

The nurse asked for the reason for my visit, and I wept. She gave me tissues. I couldn't stop. I gave her a synopsis of my past week, and she listened. She typed more notes into the computer, and she gave me a hospital gown. I changed into the gown and pushed Lorelai's stroller back and forth, back and forth, back and forth to rock her ever so slightly side to side in the hopes of lulling her asleep. I told her I needed some help and she needed to wait. She dozed in and out of consciousness.

Dr. Anne entered the office, and this time she was wearing an A-line floral dress with heels. No more scrubs. Her pretty porcelain doll face couldn't mask the look of concern she wore as she approached me. She sat on her black swivel chair and explained that the Edinburgh Postnatal Depression Scale is based on a thirty-point system. A score of zero indicates no symptoms of depression, while a score of thirty indicates the most severe display of symptoms. Any patient who scores a ten or greater is evaluated for possible postpartum depression by the health care professional. Dr. Anne told me that I scored twenty-nine points.

Almost perfect.

. . .

That night, I started bleeding. It was sudden, and I was scared.

I was scared my sutures had ripped. I was scared my intestines ruptured from the diarrhea. I was scared of going back to the hospital. I asked Noah to pray for me, and I cried to the Lord to make it stop. Lorelai wailed. It was 9:00 p.m. and Noah dialed the phone number for the on-call doctor at the maternity ward. I explained my symptoms, but I played down the amount of blood that pooled through the sanitary napkin. I couldn't go back to the hospital. I would rather die in my bathroom. It would have been a great relief. I was paralyzed by fear.

The on-call doctor advised I take Kaopectate for the diarrhea, and he explained the extra bleeding could be attributed to the abdominal palpations I received at my appointment earlier in the day. I was advised to monitor the amount of bleeding, and to go to the emergency room if it continued. Noah left to buy the medicine, and I nursed Lorelai to stop her wails. My uterus contracted, and a prune-sized blood clot appeared. The bleeding slowed. I gulped mouthfuls of the chalky liquid Noah brought me which I convinced myself would be the answer to my prayers.

I dozed in and out of sleep for two hours, until Lorelai cried to be nursed. Then another two hours in bed. Nurse. Two hours. Nurse. Trips to the bathroom occurred hourly. The sun appeared once again, and Noah left for work. I convinced myself everything was fine. I convinced myself I didn't need anyone else. I swallowed my newly prescribed Zoloft and downed the remaining ounces of Kaopectate in my desperation to stop the burning in my stomach. I nibbled on dry toast and bananas, and I could see my body shrink. My wedding ring was loose, and my cheekbones had reappeared. Lorelai slept for long stretches, but my thoughts kept me awake.

I prayed in constant desperation. I listened to worship music and cried to the Lord. On the couch. On the floor. In my bed, the kitchen, and the bathroom. I meditated on the Scripture from Paul, a man comfortable with being uncomfortable:

> "Do not be anxious about anything, but in everything by prayer and supplication with thanksgiving let your requests be made known to God. And the peace of

God, which surpasses all understanding, will guard your hearts and minds in Christ Jesus."
Philippians 4:6-7 (ESV)

I searched the Scriptures for some piece I had missed — when will the peace of God come to me? When will *my* healing occur? Where could I go for rest? I had no answers to endless questions. I received texts and cards from well-intentioned friends who joked about their memories of caring for a newborn– skipping showers, skipping meals, finding sleep at odd times. They didn't mention anything about recurring flashbacks to a traumatic birth. They didn't mention visions of throwing the baby out the window. They didn't mention any rehospitalization or resigning themselves to bleed out over their toilets. *Just me?* I decided it was best to not mention it either. I decided to tell them everything was fine.

CHAPTER 6
April Eighth

April 8th was a Sunday. I was three weeks postpartum, and I wanted to die. I never knew I could be so ill. My eyes could no longer focus, and I shook from anxiety. I was very thin and my body hurt. My stomach hurt. My back hurt. My breasts hurt. The volume in my ears was turned up, and I could hear everything. Mom ears. We moved Lorelai's bed from our bedroom to the hallway. Our apartment's 900 square feet made it easy to hear every wiggle or squeak that came out of that purple Pack n' Play. I wanted to turn down the volume in my mind, but I couldn't. A digital watch in our bedroom beeped on the top of every hour, and I grew more anxious with each reminder that I had lost yet another hour of sleep.

I dreaded the night.

That morning, I walked to the kitchen to pour fresh water into the 40-ounce plastic jug which never left my side. I shoved three probiotic tablets into my mouth, along with the Zoloft I prayed would take effect sooner than later. My hands shook the jug. I grabbed an apple from the refrigerator. It was the only food that looked appealing. I took a small bite and chew, chew, chewed. When it came time to swallow, my stomach gurgled. I had to eat. I had to have something. Anything. I forced it down, but it was instantly rejected with an explosion of water, undigested white and yellow tablets, and apple pulp which spread over the stovetop, down the sides, and into those plastic air vents attached to the oven. Those would be hard to clean. I slumped down to the floor. Dizzy. I sat on the cheap gray linoleum that caught my same tears ten months ago. Those tears came after seeing the tiny plus sign on the pregnancy test. That was a moment of joy.

Now, everything was different.

Everything.

I asked Him to take my life. I did not want to live one more minute in this reality. I no longer cared that I was given a child. I wanted somebody, anybody, to take her and let me run away into a new state. A new country. Another world. Anywhere but here. I spent the last two weeks wiping the putrid shame I could not control off of the toilet, the bathroom floor, my clothes, my towels and my legs. Lorelai began to wail for her first feed of the day, and I woke Noah up to help. I told him I couldn't feed her anymore. I could no longer feed myself. He picked up Lorelai who fell asleep on his warm chest and strong arms. *Daddy*.

We made a plan.

I sipped on a cup of whole milk. I was so nauseated, but I knew I needed to force down the calories. It stayed down. I fed Lorelai, and Noah asked me to try and sleep in the bedroom.

"I can't sleep," I told him.

"You need to try," he responded. "You have to keep trying. I will take Lorelai. I will watch her all day, and I'll only wake you up when she needs to eat. I promise, it'll be fine. It'll be fun. I love holding her. It's my favorite."

I went to the bedroom to try and force myself to sleep. I tried deep breathing. Prayer. White noise machine. Fluff the pillow. Un-fluff the pillow. Read a book. Put the book down. Darken the curtains. Lay on my right side. Lay on my left side. Stomach, back, stomach, back. Over and over I turned like a gas station hot dog that was left on the coils too long. It was maddening. I pushed the bedroom door open to see Noah sitting on our gray chair with Lorelai sleeping on his shoulder. Watching golf. Playing chess on his iPhone. *How could he be so happy?*

I plopped on the floor next to him, and I put my head on his knees.

"I can't sleep," I groaned. "I can't do this. I can't do this. I can't eat, I can't sleep. I can't do it. I can't go on."

My eyes couldn't focus on his face. They darted back and forth. Up and down. Like a rogue pinball machine, my eyes searched and searched and searched for something to fix this feeling, something new to turn back time. It became impossible to get a deep breath. My heart beat reverberated in my ears, but everything else buzzed with a manic electricity. Rational thoughts disappeared. *This is it. This is the end. It's over; I'm done.*

"Lisa!" Noah's commanding voice brought me back to the present. "Everything is going to be O.K. This is really hard right now. What you are experiencing is a panic attack. I can see it start when you breathe faster, you pick at your skin, and your eyes go a little crazy. If you just breathe, your liver will filter out all the chemicals that are making you feel this way. This is going to sound crazy, but try to enjoy the feeling and think of it as something that will go away soon. We can probably set a timer for three minutes and it will be over."

"Really?" I responded. I should have been able to recognize the symptoms, but I had gotten used to the feeling. The electricity.

He asked me if any food sounded good to me? *No.* Could I try and sleep again? *No. I couldn't.* Would it help to get out of the apartment? *I don't know. I don't know. I just don't know.*

Noah decided for me that it would be a good idea to get out of the apartment. I put together a diaper back for Lorelai, but I was nervous to leave. I was afraid of being away from my bathroom. I didn't want to be out where there wasn't a toilet close by. I was terrified by the thought of the rest of the day. *What if she needs to eat when we are out? When will she need to nap? What if she cries the whole time? Should I just stay here and try to sleep?*

I came back to the living room in tears. Again.

"I can't do this!" I cried. "I cannot keep going! What will my body do if it doesn't fall asleep? What will happen if I can't eat *any* food?"

I sat to his left on the couch, and I stared down into my reflection on the black glass coffee table. My head in my hands, I looked in my eyes as if seeing a stranger. Who am I?

"Jesus help me! Jesus help me!" I called out, "Please, do something. I need you, I need you, I need you! Please do something! Please save me! Oh, Jesus you have to save me!"

I had never felt such desperation. It was life or death. A song from our old church in Nashville came to my mind.

> "Just a touch of the hem of your garment,
> Let us be healed,
> Let us be free.
> Just a touch can restore us to wholeness,
> Lord we believe,
> Lord we believe."
>
> The Anchor Fellowship (2008)

Noah prayed with me, and we cried together. I shook back and forth, and back and forth and I could feel the tears drip down. It was a bitter moment. Torment. I began to journal that day, because I knew I would want to remember the Lord's answer to my prayer. I knew it was something I would need to remember.

APRIL 8, 2018 @ 1:00 PM
I came to the Lord through the power of the Holy Spirit and he has DECLARED that He works all things together for the GOOD of those who LOVE Him. Satan's trying to take me out. But I am victorious. I am full of righteous anger at his lies & his schemes. I am VICTORIOUS in Jesus. I will worry about NOTHING but in everything through prayer and supplication I will present my requests to the Lord & He will give me the peace which surpasses understanding.

    I am a leader in the church, and Satan wants me to stop but I will stand victorious. DO NOT WORRY. No details, just don't worry. My spirit is willing though my flesh is weak. The Lord will allow me to live outside of the physical realm & I will dwell in the shelter of the most high God. NO PLAGUE will come near my tent. The Lord gave me a vision of the peace I've been begging for — He is not gently holding me BUT He is raging & battling in front of me. He has a shield in front of me & I must simply stand. His anger burns on my behalf.

    I will not be taken out. I will stand indignant against the schemes of the evil one. Fear NOT. Period.

APRIL 8 @ 4:00
Dad speak to me. I'm weak. I can't eat or sleep. This is how David felt at times too. He spent time in anguish as I am. I feel lonely. Lord, come & heal me. Jesus is King of Kings. I am a weak slave, but you must give me your SUPERNATURAL strength to overcome. Give me rest. Give me sleep specifically. Relieve my stomach nausea. Lord take it away. Laughter is the best medicine — Dad give me laughter. This too shall pass. Amen Jesus.

• • •

That afternoon we drove to GNC and bought a weight-gain protein supplement to increase my caloric intake. I picked the chocolate flavor. Always go for the chocolate. Lorelai cried when we tried to strap her in the car seat. She hated to be in the car, and she let us know. I couldn't blame her. I wouldn't want to be in a car seat either. We drove to Meijer, and Noah put any food in the basket that I thought sounded appealing. We walked to the check-out lanes, and I had to go to the bathroom. Now. I waddled briskly to the ladies' room, and I prayed I wouldn't poop my pants in the middle of a hustling grocery crowd on a Sunday afternoon. I made it, but I was in so much pain.

I walked out of the bathroom and into the car, and Noah asked me if any food sounded good to me. Anything. I looked around, and I saw a handful of fast food restaurants I hadn't visited in years.

"Hamburger," I decided.

I hadn't eaten a fast-food hamburger in as long as I could remember, but it sounded good. I asked for a burger with pickles, ketchup, lettuce, and tomato. I opened the cardboard box, and a wave of nausea hit me. *Just a bite. I just have to eat one bite.* I got it down. I drank some water. I started to cry.

"I can't do it," I said. "I can't sleep. I can't eat. I'm not going to make it. I'm not going to make it!"

"Lisa," Noah spoke. "You will be O.K. This will be over soon. One day you will look back at today and be like, 'Dude, that was the worst!', but it won't last forever. We'll go home. You can lay down and rest, and I can keep an eye on Lorelai. Sound O.K.?"

"O.K." I trusted his ability to form a good plan. I didn't trust mine. I was too sick.

* * *

We prayed together on the drive home. I fed Lorelai, and Noah made me a milkshake with ice cream, whole milk, weight-gainer protein powder, and peanut butter. I sipped. The nausea was constant. I couldn't take any more than that first bite of hamburger. No other solid food would stay down. I knew that if I ate, I could sleep. I also knew that if I slept, things would seem better. I tried to lay down, but my body shook. I ran to the bathroom. Lots of pain. I became frantic. My mind was out of control. I couldn't think straight.

My new life felt like a treadmill I was locked into. Every day I got weaker. Every day I had to run faster. More of me was required every day, but I had nothing to give. I couldn't seem to catch my breath. There was no option to stop or let go. *Even if I could slow down, how could I ever catch up on sleep? How could my body ever recover from this? What will happen tomorrow? How will I make it to Friday? And next week, will it be worse? Am I going to die? Are my intestines going to explode? Will I get another infection and die?* Round and round the questions swirled with no respite. More than anything else, I was afraid of having to leave home. I couldn't go back to the hospital.

I had to stay here. At home.

I explained my treadmill analogy to Noah. He suggested I try to use the breast pump, and he could start to bottle feed Lorelai in the night.

"I don't want to make you do that," I responded with instant guilt. "It's my job. You have to get up and work. It's too much for you."

"No, it's not," he responded. "If it was too much for me, I would tell you it was too much. I'll sleep here on the couch, then I can be closest to her when she cries. I'll feed her a bottle, and you can sleep in the bedroom. You need to let me do this."

"But I can't sleep!" I told him.

"Well, you have to try," he reminded me. "And at least if you are in bed, your body is resting. You will sleep, eventually your body will fall asleep."

I agreed. I knew he was right. I watched the breast pump as it stretched and contorted my body. *This is weird. Really weird.* About an ounce of what looked like cloudy water was the result. I sipped on my milkshake. I switched sides, and got a similar result. Noah then asked me to try and sleep while I had the chance. I tried. Then I paced from our bedroom to our living room and wiped down the kitchen counters for the seventeenth time. I panicked. My chest tightened. I couldn't see straight. My ears buzzed.

I have to stop breastfeeding. I have to stop. I can't give any more.

I walked to the couch and announced to Noah, "I think I have to stop breastfeeding."

"Oh," he responded with a surprised look.

"I know!" I cried. "I know we've never talked about it before. I'm really sorry. I'm so sorry. I just can't."

"Well, you know I want to support you 100%," he said. "What about using the breast pump? If you make the bottles, I can give them to her. And other people could help feed her too."

"No." *I just can't. I have nothing left. Will Noah think I'm a bad mom? Will Lorelai be healthy with formula? Is it expensive? Like, really expensive? What if she won't take a bottle? What if she won't drink it? What if it hurts her stomach?*

"I'm so sorry. Are you disappointed in me?" I asked him.

"Ha! Disappointed? Are you kidding me? No. Absolutely not. You are a champion. I just don't know anything about formula," he spoke with reassurance.

"Me either! I have no idea! I know I just can't keep going!" I broke down into tears.

I thought of my friend Sandra. She had a baby recently, her second child. We knew each other through work, and she had been checking in on me and Lorelai nearly every day. We sent each other pictures of our newborn babies, and she let me ask as many questions as I wanted about the color and texture of the stuff I found in Lorelai's diapers. You know you have a good friend when you can compare poopy diaper notes. She had chosen to stop breastfeeding both of her children earlier than recommended, and I knew she would be honest with me. I video-called her on FaceTime, and she answered right away.

"Hi Lisa!" she answered with her usual friendliness, but then she could see my face. She could see the tears and the puffy eyes and the disappointment. I couldn't stop the tears. I told her I thought I needed to switch to formula, but I didn't know anything about it. I explained that I didn't think I had the physical health to continue to breastfeed. I was depleted.

She told me *fed* is best. She showed me her three-year-old daughter running circles around the living room and laughing. She told me she was *thriving*. She showed me her newborn son, asleep in his bassinet. He looked so strong. *He's thriving.* Sandra reminded me that I had to take care of myself. If I didn't, I couldn't take care of the baby. It was like the airplane flight attendant telling me how to apply my own oxygen mask. Then I could give the lifesaving air to my child. But if I didn't? If I didn't, we would both be in trouble.

Noah and I agreed I would go to buy baby formula first thing tomorrow morning. He asked if I could try to use the breast pump again so that there would be enough for a feeding during the night. He said he would give her the bottle. Relief flooded my mind. She wouldn't be dependent on my body for her life. My body was a void. My mind churned with guilt. ...*I am the one who is supposed to be up at night, not Noah. I am the one who* is supposed to do the feeding. This was the one thing I could do right, and I'm done already? How will he be able to go to work in the mornings if he feeds her two or three times in the night? Would he resent me for this?

I knew I needed more help. My mom had called me each day since Lorelai's birth to check on "the girls." She always offered to drive to Ohio at any time if I needed her help. I brushed off the offers. I had wanted to do it by myself. I wanted to do it all. I had a plan. I had a picture in my mind of how I would be as a "stay-at-home" mom, and it didn't include me asking for help. If other people could do it on their own, then I could too. I grasped for that abstract prize of martyrdom that other mothers seemed to achieve through lost hours of sleep and cold cups of coffee.

I walked to the laundry room. It was just big enough for one person to stand between the washer and dryer units we rented for $30 a month. The washer was old and convulsed violently with every load. The dryer required two or three cycles to do its job. I dialed my mom's phone number as I leaned on a pile of towels that were dry but disheveled. When she answered the phone with her usual chipper tone, I broke into tears once again. *Why is it so hard to ask for help?* I told her I needed someone to stay with me when Noah was gone. I told her I was in a crisis. I told her I didn't know how long I needed her to stay.

Even though my mom had retired from her nursing career years ago, she still had that kind of voice that I'm certain she used in the ICU. It wasn't sympathetic necessarily, but it was intentional. It was full of reassurance and confidence. She was a rescuer. A helper. She knew I needed someone who could withstand my swirling storm of emotions without being caught up in the madness. She was full of hope. She gathered the facts and repeated them back to me for accuracy. She agreed to drive to Ohio as soon as possible, and to stay as long as I needed.

"Thank you for asking me," she said. She could sense the mom guilt in me. "I am glad you asked me. I am happy to help you, whatever you need. Sometimes you just need your mother to be there and not ask any questions. You don't have to explain anything. I will be there. Help is on the way."

That was that. A plan was in place. A change was inevitable. This relentless cycle of crying and insomnia and pain and sickness would end. I knew that it may not get easier anytime soon, but at least it would be different. I would be able to stop breastfeeding. I would be able to hand my child off to my mother during the day. I still saw no light at the end of the tunnel, but it was just enough hope to take one more step. One more moment. One more day.

> "O Lord, how long will you forget me? Forever?
> How long will you look the other way?
> How long must I struggle with anguish in my soul,
> With sorrow in my heart every day?
> How long will my enemy have the upper hand?
> Turn and answer me, O Lord my God!
> Restore the sparkle to my eyes, or I will die."
> Psalms 13: 1-3 (NLT)

CHAPTER 7
Breast is Best

I stared at all the posters in the obstetrics department during my pregnancy visits. I read all the statistics. I had it all planned out. I planned to breastfeed for a year. I was in awe of breastfeeding. It was amazing. God gave me a built-in feeding station which functioned with no conscientious effort on my part. I knew that if I fed myself well and drank a lot of water, I could trust my body to turn that into a ready-made meal for my child. It hurt at first. A lot. They say that it shouldn't hurt if you do it right. They don't tell you that it may take a while to do it right. Lorelai and I had to learn together. We were both new to this. I knew breastfeeding was objectively superior.

I knew it was the best.

Even the canisters of baby formula reminded me: "IMPORTANT NOTICE: BREAST MILK IS BEST FOR BABIES.[3]" I stared at the cans and bottles and boxes of baby formula on a sloppy Monday morning. April 9th. It was raining. I had Lorelai with me. Noah had bottle fed her a pumped bottle of breastmilk for the first feeding of the prior night. He said she took it after a couple moments of confusion. She's so smart. I knew it. I grabbed a generic-looking formula that seemed to be a popular choice and threw it in the cart. I was nauseated, and had to rush to the bathroom.

I continued to waste away over the toilet. I couldn't wake up from this nightmare. I cried with muffled tears in the handicap stall while Lorelai sat in her car seat in front of me. Her presence was constant, yet I felt so alone. The treadmill continued to zoom faster and faster.

> "For my groaning comes out at the sight of my food,
> And my cries pour out like water.
> For what I dread befalls me.
> I am not at ease, nor am I quiet,
> And I am not at rest, but turmoil comes."
> Job 3:24-25 (NASB)

"Hi! Are you alone today?" the text message read.

It was from Megan. We had volunteered together the past few years in our church's high school ministry. Every Sunday night during the school year, Megan and I met with a small group of high school girls in her basement to talk about the Bible and walk through life together. They ate popcorn and laughed and cried, and it was an honor to help point them to Christ. Megan had brought meals to me during my pregnancy. Lasagna. Chicken pot pie. Love in a casserole dish. She was the one I called when I was encouraged to pursue an induction. She was the one who prayed with me over the phone.

"Yes." I responded. I was so alone.

"I just so happen to be working from home today! How about I bring my laptop to you, and I can work at your apartment. What do you want me to bring you for lunch? Does anything sound good?"

My eyes teared up immediately. It became obvious to me that the Lord put me on Megan's heart at this moment of great loneliness. When I was too afraid to ask for help, the Lord brought the help to me. I sat in the car in the parking lot of our apartment complex. Lorelai had fallen asleep in her car seat, so I kept the motor on and listened to the radio. Her box of formula stared at me from the passenger seat. My breasts hurt, but I wanted to wait as long as I could to pump. Today I started to wean myself off milk production. "Drying out," they call it.

I texted Megan that a plain turkey sandwich sounded edible. She knew my current health and mental condition, so she knew it wasn't safe for me to be alone with my own thoughts. She knew she needed to step in, instead of waiting for me to ask for help. She loved without invitation. When Lorelai began to stir, I walked with her up our three flights of stairs. I kept her in her car seat while I mixed a scoop and a half of powder into three ounces of water. I warmed it for a couple of minutes in a hot mug of water. The powdered formula didn't smell good.

I sat with Lorelai on the couch. Now I had to figure out how to hold her while I also held the bottle. More new things I knew nothing about. God was merciful, and she gulped down her bottle and gave me a hearty burp. A few drops of the formula fell out of the side of her mouth, but she fell asleep immediately. She looked so calm and content. I was relieved. I used the breast pump, and put the bottle in the refrigerator. I planned to give her pumped milk every other feeding before switching to formula entirely. It looked weird in the fridge. It gave a whole new meaning to the term "leftovers."

I put Lorelai in her pink rocker. She was so good at sleeping. Megan knocked on our door, and I was no longer alone. Like a bright little match in the dark cavern of my mind, she stood in the doorway with food and hugs and hope. She set up her laptop on my kitchen table, and she held Lorelai in her lap. She made me try to eat, even though I told her I couldn't. I had two bites, and it stayed down. We both celebrated.

I knew at that moment that the worst was over.

Help was here.

I could keep down food, regardless of how little it was. I wasn't knocked out of the ring yet. I gulped water and had a sip of the weight-gainer shake Noah had made for me the night before. The worst was over. I knew it.

> "But they who wait for the Lord shall renew their strength; they shall mount up with wings like eagles; they shall run and not be weary; they shall walk and not faint."
>
> Isaiah 40:31 (ESV)

Megan stayed with me until 5:00 that night. She changed diapers and took conference calls. She got me to eat the whole sandwich. Something in her presence calmed me just enough to keep food down. She read notes on her laptop and gave Lorelai her bottles. She burped her and talked to her and gave her the nurturing touch she needed that day. She asked me to try and sleep, and I tried without success. The electricity was still turned on high. I continued to have diarrhea, but it was not as frequent. Megan cooked dinner for Noah and I. Barbecued meatballs. I ate two. She loved without hesitation. She gave without expecting anything in return.

And that is how I survived that day.

CHAPTER 8
Help

My mom texted me the next morning at 6:00 a.m.

"Leaving the driveway! The troops are coming!"

She arrived at our apartment before noon and knocked gently on the door. I opened it to see mom in her standard outfit: a pastel colored cardigan over a coordinating collared shirt. Black slacks with an elastic waistband. Hairspray held each blonde strand in perfect position. She smelled like bar soap and warmth and fabric softener. Mom gave off an air of confidence and determination as she stepped in our apartment to begin her week of tending to my hot mess. Lorelai was asleep in her pink rocker. She was the best baby. I just couldn't see it.

Yet.

• • •

I took a long shower. I allowed my mind to go numb from the pain and stress of my reality. As I wiped the condensation off of the mirror, I gasped at the woman who stared back at me. This stranger in the mirror was not me. She stared back with frantic eyes. The infection and sickness left her body pale and bony. There was no light in her eyes, and there was no laughter in her life. She looked pitiful. Everything felt pitiful.

Mom and I ate lunch. It didn't sit well, but at least it was down. I used the breast pump next. Lorelai had taken her bottles like a champion, to my great relief. She had formula every other feeding with no protest. My mom suggested I take Tulip out for a short walk. Fresh air and a change of scenery. It was surreal. It felt so good to be *alone*. To walk the dog. It was something familiar, and I knew how to do it. I didn't have to think or plan or struggle. I took my time. I envied the neighbors driving in and out of the apartment complex just like they did any other Tuesday afternoon. As if their life hadn't changed overnight. As if their lives weren't shaken to pieces like a broken ship in a bottle.

My mom could see me struggle with panic attacks and bouts of crying. She held my hand when I fell apart, like she did decades ago. She looked into my eyes with worry until I could stop shaking. Until I could breathe. She asked if I wanted to get out of the apartment by myself, but I just couldn't. The thought of driving in the car and functioning in the general public seemed monumentally impossible. I was so tired. Too tired. I tried to sleep, but I couldn't. Mom took care of Lorelai's diaper changes and her next feeding. She did the laundry and cleaned the kitchen and we watched *The Great British Baking Show* on Netflix.

When Noah came home from work, my mom went to get carry-out dinner. Greek food. I ate some. Mom asked if my diarrhea had stopped since she arrived. It had not. Noah took the role of baby whisperer when Lorelai started her evening grumpy time. She was so loud when she cried, even as a newborn. So loud. Noah walked up and down the hallway with Lorelai's face in front of his own. He sang "L-O-V-E." a half a dozen times until Lorelai had calmed down enough to take a pacifier and nod off. When mom got her jacket on to head back to her hotel for the night, I couldn't breathe. I hated the night.

I began to cry while I sat in the rocking chair. I couldn't hold it in. I was afraid Lorelai wouldn't sleep that night. I was afraid Noah would get sick from exhaustion and not be able to work. I was afraid I wouldn't be able to sleep. I was afraid Lorelai would get sick after being weaned off of breastmilk. I was afraid I would stay sick. I was afraid this reality was my new forever.

"Lisa," mom told me as she grabbed my shoulders that shook the rocking chair. "It's over. The worst is over. You don't have to go back and do it again. It's over."

I didn't realize I was afraid of reliving the past three weeks, but she was right. Time marches forward, not backward. I didn't have to go back to that hospital room on the fourth floor with the nurses standing around me with their hands ready for something I could never have prepared for. I remembered how bright the lights shone during the delivery. It was blinding. As my mom held my shoulders that couldn't stop shaking, God gave me a vision. I looked down into that delivery room while angels circled the hospital bed with song and with prayer. A holy heaviness filled their eyes. I could see myself with feet in stirrups and my head straining forward in breathless agony. I could see Noah next to me. My hand was held in his.

It was over. I didn't have to go back.

> "I am with you and will watch over you wherever you go, and I will bring you back to this land.
> I will not leave you until I have done what I have promised you."
>
> Genesis 28:15 (NIV)

"Does this get any easier?? Please tell me it gets easier."

I had sent that text to my friend Alice a week after Lorelai was born. We had been coworkers for the previous two years, and she told me about the difficulties she experienced after the births of her children. We would walk and talk during breaks, and she always spoke with unapologetic honesty. She could always make me laugh.

"Lisa. What is going on? Are you O.K.? The transition to this parenthood gig is the most difficult transition you'll have to face. I know. I've been there. I'll shoot you straight."

Something in her words gave me the freedom to spill all of my pain onto her. I knew she would understand. I knew I didn't have to explain what I couldn't understand myself. I told her about the rehospitalization, the insomnia, the diarrhea, the fear. I told her the doctors recommended I continue to breastfeed, and I told her I chose to stop. I told her I had no desire to be with my baby. I felt no love or compassion when I saw her. I was afraid of her. I couldn't wake up from my nightmare. I couldn't keep going.

"I get it. Listen, I have been there. I am going to walk with you through this, literally and figuratively. When is the earliest you would feel up to meeting?"

Wednesday, April 11th was the first warm day in such a long time. A lifetime. It was one of those days that caught me by surprise. My mom arrived early that morning to help with Lorelai. Once they were comfortably situated in our living room, I drove to Sharon Woods to meet Alice. We needed to take a walk. She hugged me the moment I stepped out of my car, and she handed me a pink gift bag stuffed with neon tissue paper, a necklace and flowers. Everything was so pretty. Everything was bright. We began our walk towards the lake. We took it slow and stopped to look at the lounging turtles and hidden waterfalls along the trail. She made me laugh. She took all the pressure off of me.

Eventually, I confessed to her that I wanted to go back in time. I was regretful. I wanted to have made different decisions. I wanted to take it all back. The pregnancy. All the changes. I told her I was overwhelmed with guilt as I listened to Noah taking care of Lorelai at odd hours, but not me. Not me. I could only lay in bed and shake and cry and race to the toilet. I acted like a robot towards my own daughter: feed her, burp her, change her, dress her, put her down. Repeat. Repeat. Repeat. I didn't want to hold her, I wanted her to go away. In my mind, I thought I had reached a dead end. I thought it would be miserable from here on out. There was no hope.

Then, when I finished talking, Alice told me her story. She didn't hold anything back. I learned about the difficulties she experienced after having both of her children. I could not believe this successful, nurturing, passionate woman had been pulled down into the same murky whirlpool of postpartum depression I found myself drowning in. Her story was raw and messy, but it immediately brought a quiet calm to my mind. Hope existed, and she was the living proof. I knew her and I knew her children. I had seen how much they loved, and even liked, each other. I couldn't believe it.

Could that be me?

There was no talk of overnight fixes. She validated my overwhelming feelings of all-consuming guilt that accompanies postpartum depression. She told me she also suffered from insomnia during her first weeks postpartum. It wasn't until she was prescribed medication that she was able to sleep and think clearly. She didn't have an instant love connection with her child either. It grew slowly. She was honest with me about what lay ahead: a lot of work. Time needed to pass — separation between myself and the birth. I needed to allow my mind to forget. She told me the best thing I could do for my daughter was to take care of myself. She assured me that bonding would eventually come. It may not be for a while, and that is O.K. She told me I was a good mom.

None of the words she said made any of the problems go away. I still lived in the same reality, but I now saw some flickering light at the end of a very long and dark tunnel. I didn't care how dim it appeared, it was a light and it was real. I knew I had to run towards that glow with all my strength and to not slow down until I reached it. I drove home to find my mom on the porch, with Lorelai on her lap. She was wrapped snug and soft as the gentlest rays of sun kissed her sweet little face. It was good. I took a breath and stood in the sun. It seemed like a lifetime since I had felt such warmth.

> "The light shines in the darkness, and the darkness has not overcome it."
> John 1:5 (NIV)

Ruth was a friendly face I had passed in the church hallways every now and again, but I didn't know much about her. She led the Mom's Group at our church, a community which met weekly during the school years to provide support and sanity to both new and veteran mothers. After I left the hospital for the second time, she had sent me an email to ask if I wanted to set up a "meal train." I didn't know what a meal train was *exactly*, but I anticipated we would receive a few casseroles or frozen dishes from well-wishing families at our church. I struggled to find an appetite, but I knew it would be helpful to have food ready for Noah when he returned home from work.

I answered her questions regarding food preferences and provided my contact information. Within an hour I began to receive emails from the meal train website, notifying me that people had signed up to take me a meal. I logged in, and I was shocked. Ruth had set up a plan for meals to be delivered to our apartment every Monday, Wednesday, and Friday for the next six weeks.

That was a lot more than a few casseroles. An option to donate money to our family was available to help cover the extra expenses following childbirth. Two people had already donated. Names appeared on the assigned dates that I didn't recognize. New names meant someone I hadn't even met would cook my family dinner, drive it across town, and walk up our three flights of stairs and into my life. These names were people who didn't know my story, but they knew what it was like to have a newborn baby. It was hard, and I needed help.

Ruth was the first person to bring us a meal. I opened the door to see her holding a big Bob Evans paper bag in one hand, still steaming from the pounds of hot turkey and mashed potatoes, and a vase of flowers in the other hand. She explained to me that, "sometimes it helps to have something nice to look at during times like these."

It really does.

She placed the bag of food on the kitchen counter and washed her hands. It's the thing to do with new babies. It was about 5:00 p.m., and Lorelai was starting to fuss. She squirmed and cried and the dog barked. Noise everywhere. Ruth sat and offered to hold Lorelai for a bit so I could rest. As I watched her pick up my tiny daughter and hold her as if she was her own, I could see that this was something she had done hundreds of times before.

"So, how are you doing?" She looked at me with a confident and soft eye contact that seemed to read my mind before I could respond. "Sometimes it's easier to open up to a stranger about these kinds of things instead of a family member."

She patted Lorelai's back and rocked ever so slightly side to side.

Can I trust her? With this?? I don't even know her.

It took a quick moment of deliberation in my mind to determine that Ruth was indeed a safe place for me. She showed me in her actions that she was on our team — organizing meals, rallying support, and being the first to serve. I had nothing to offer her but my story. I spoke to her through tears and exhaustion. She never interrupted, and she never lost eye contact. She listened in a way that made me feel as if I was the only person in the world that existed to her at that moment. She didn't offer suggestions. She simply allowed a patient silence to exist until I was able to form my next thought.

She put Lorelai in my arms, and she fell asleep immediately. Her tiny hand with the pink fingernails went limp on my shoulder.

"She knows her Mommy," she told me. "Look at that. She's so relaxed. She just needed her Mommy."

It was true.

"O.K., Lisa," she began. "This is a very difficult situation, but it will be fine. I promise. Keep letting Noah help you. Keep taking your medication. Make sure you don't miss a doctor appointment. There are hundreds of people praying for you. There are hundreds of people here to help you. Whenever you think you can't handle Lorelai anymore, just bring her to my house for however long you need. Start to write out all your thoughts. It doesn't matter if you burn the notebooks after, just keep writing and writing until there are no words left."

The help didn't stop there. I needed more, and more was provided. The meal train became a source of strength in more ways than one. There were nights Julie brought grilled chicken and a whole watermelon cut into perfect squares. She sat with me and talked to me for hours until Noah came home from work. Tina and Alan came to our apartment and prayed over us and held Lorelai, who cried and cried. Missy and Mick stopped by with a tray of ham sandwiches on sweet Hawaiian rolls. Heather brought soup and salad and six different kinds of cupcakes. Sara came with Chris and a crock pot full of chicken with rice. I didn't know Alicia, but she drove across town with four kids in her car and homemade chicken tikka masala and jasmine rice just for us. I hadn't met Terra, but she cooked her favorite spaghetti casserole and drove thirty minutes with her three children to deliver it.

These were moms who knew what I needed without having to ask. These were moms who were filled with the love of Christ, and as far as they were concerned, we were all family.

CHAPTER 9
Emergency

April 16, 2018 was a Monday. Lorelai was one day short of her first month's birthday.

Happy Birthday, baby.

I didn't feel good. I felt sweaty and sore. My back hurt. My stomach hurt. Everything seemed to ache. Lorelai was established on formula, and I had "dried out." She showed no changes since I stopped breastfeeding. I felt less anxiety with each day of using formula. Breast is best, but formula was freedom. Our air conditioning broke the day my mom went home to Tennessee. Then again two days later. Noah's paternal grandmother, "Grandma Hardwick" made a plan to visit us the following day. I was thankful to have a constant presence of people at home while I was with Lorelai. It helped me stay out of my brain.

I took my temperature and it beeped at 100.4 degrees.

That's not normal.

Nothing is normal.

. . .

I called the obstetrics office and made an immediate appointment for what I convinced myself was a run-of-the-mill urinary tract infection. I thought it could be a result of the diarrhea which had slowed down to eight to ten times a day. After I stopped breastfeeding, I was able to take Imodium. It took the edge off.

It no longer woke me up at night, and I felt safe enough to drive where I needed to go with Lorelai and not worry about a toilet being too far away. It was good enough for me. I had hope.

I brought Lorelai with me to the appointment. She squirmed and protested in the waiting room. I tried to rock her, give her a pacifier, roll the stroller gently forward and backward, forward and backward. She didn't care. She cried all the same, but it didn't make the nurse call my name any quicker. She cried because she needed love and attention, but she had no idea how to express it in words. She cried because she was tired and alone. She cried because she didn't know where she was or what was going to happen. Me too, baby.

I reviewed my symptoms for the umpteenth time with the nurse practitioner. I felt like my whole self was just a list of symptoms.

"How many times a day do you have diarrhea?" she asked, clicking coded notes about me that I would never be allowed to see. She seemed concerned.

"Eight or so. But it's way better now! It used to be thirty," I replied.

"That's too many," she informed me. I had assumed as much.

"Well I have insomnia too. I can't sleep more than a few hours a day." I added. "I know it's from all the stress."

Words melted into tears.

"You have to get more sleep than that," she told me. As if I didn't know this already.

When I sheepishly told her I had decided to stop breast-feeding because of these symptoms, her concern morphed into disappointment. She didn't reply to me with words, but her eyes told the message she wanted me to hear.

Breast is best. No excuses.

She checked to make sure my lady parts were still healing safely. She prescribed 10 doses of Xanax to help me sleep, and she ordered a urine culture to check for a urinary tract infection. She gave me a sealed plastic bag full of sterilized equipment so that I could collect a stool sample to test for parasites. She moved up my appointment with the psychiatrist so that I would be seen sooner. I was advised to monitor my temperature, which seemed to rest right at 100 degrees. The results for the urinary tract infection culture would be available in the next few days. It was all too much. I cried so often, I assumed it was my new state of being. I put the sealed bag into Lorelai's stroller. I folded up my prescription for Xanax and stuffed it into her diaper bag. I said YES and THANK YOU and got into the elevator and walked out the door.

* * *

My fever rose by the afternoon, despite Advil and Tylenol every four hours. At 4:00 it was 101.4 degrees. I called the obstetrics office and spoke with the nurse on call. I asked about my appointment that morning: did anyone know why this was happening? What is going on in my body? She said she would send a note to the nurse practitioner I met with, and she would try to respond before 5:00 p.m. when the office closed. I cried and cried. I told her I was scared. She told me she would try and find answers as soon as she could.

At 4:30 I called again. No news.

At 4:45 I called. No news.

At 4:55 the nurse called back. She told me to go to the emergency room. Now.

Lorelai was on a blanket on the floor. She liked to kick her legs around. It was a soft plush material with lilac polka dots. We had to leave again. When would I be back? I called Noah in hysterics. He ended his session at work to meet me at the hospital. I called Stephanie to see if she could meet us at the hospital to take Lorelai home. At one month old, she didn't have the ideal immune system built up for an emergency room. Stephanie used that magic nurse voice that she had developed over decades of caring for patients. It was strong and reassuring. She said I would be fine. She said everything would be O.K. I believed her.

Lorelai didn't like being pulled from her blanket freedom and into the car seat. I didn't like being pulled from home without knowing when I could come back. I drove to the hospital and cried sloppy prayers:

"You know what, Lord? This is just ridiculous. Whatever. Whatever. Seriously. I don't care anymore. I just don't care. I can't care. This is so stupid. I don't get it! I don't care anymore. It's almost funny at this point. I'm so done. Take it all. Please. Just help me. Please."

Indescribable peace took over. I sat in the midst of my tears and imperfections and weaknesses, and God gave me freedom from the chaos.

> "And the peace of God, which surpasses all understanding, will guard your hearts and your minds in Christ Jesus."
> Philippians 4:7 (ESV)

When I arrived at the hospital, I kept Lorelai in her car seat and then buckled it into the stroller. I put a gray fabric cover over the exposed part of the car seat to block her from the cold breezes and sneezing strangers. I didn't know what to tell the employee at the registration office when she asked me why I was there.

"Umm…well I have this fever. And I just had a baby here. See? She's here. Yes. And I went to the doctor this morning. But then I called the nurse like an hour ago and then the nurse told me to come here. So, I'm here…" I explained with the mental clarity that only a hormonal and sleep-deprived new mother could muster.

She typed "fever" into the computer.

The emergency room waiting area was graciously sparse. I pushed the stroller to the farthest corner with the big glass wall. I had to go to the bathroom, but I thought I could wait it out. I opened the gray fabric cover, and I peeked into Lorelai's little rolling chamber of warmth and security. She was awake, but she wasn't crying. She didn't look happy, but rather inquisitive. She furled her little baby eyebrows and assessed the gleaming lights and odd sounds at this new place I had drug her to. I pushed her stroller back and forth to trick her into sleeping, but then she began to cry. As babies do. I saw Noah's black Scion pull into the parking lot, and I watched him rush from the car towards the red neon emergency room sign. He hugged me and held Lorelai. We reminded each other everything is going to be O.K.

It's going to be O.K.

Little time passed before I was given a room and instructed to put on a blue hospital robe. A balding male nurse with thick glasses arrived. He offered the usual litany of questions regarding my medical history and my current symptoms. After he recorded my vitals, he asked me if I planned to be a "stay-at-home" mom or a "working" mom.

"I plan to stay home," I replied, curious as to why he would ask that type of question in this setting.

"Both are equally difficult, in different ways," he started. "Being a mom is the hardest job of all no matter how you do it, but it is so important. You are staying home to raise your daughter? That is wonderful. She is very loved already. You are a great mom. You will never regret the time you put into teaching your children."

           • • •

The doctor ordered lab work for my blood and urine. Stephanie arrived and took Lorelai home. She reminded me everything will be O.K. As I waited, I felt my stomach churn. I threw off my blood pressure cuff and ran to the patient bathroom. I wasn't fast enough. I threw out the pair of underwear and did my best to clean up. When I came back to the room, I threw my first robe into the dirty laundry basket and tied on a new one. Fresh, muted green. I didn't go into details with Noah.

"I threw out that pair of underwear," I told him.

This was not what I had in mind when I pictured my future as a mom.

The doctor came. His hair was cut short, as if for convenience sake. He was wiry and athletic, like a grasshopper ready to pounce. He wore a big black digital watch that seemed to swallow up his wrist. He said the test was negative for a urinary tract infection, and I responded in tears. I wanted definitive answers, and I wanted them to be simple. He explained my white blood cell count was elevated, but he couldn't identify the culprit. He explained his hesitation to order antibiotics because it could further exacerbate the diarrhea. He explained the origin of the infection was indeterminable unless I chose to be admitted and undergo a CT scan and additional blood work. He explained that it was up to me, and he was sincere. I didn't know what to do with more unanswered questions, so I just cried.

I chose to go home. I was instructed to keep a close eye on all my symptoms and temperature. It hung around 100 degrees. The printed instructions told me to drink fluids, rest, take acetaminophen or ibuprofen for fever and pain; the usual routine.

I stopped at a gas station on the way home and squinted at all the different neon-colored drinks to determine which one had the best combination of electrolytes and vitamins and minerals that I could convince myself would fix everything. I was hit with the familiar burn, and I scurried to the bathroom. After a few painful minutes, I hurried to grab the closest electrolyte drink and paid without making eye contact with the clerk. I couldn't believe my own reality. I drove home and threw a frozen pizza into the oven. Nothing else sounded appetizing. I ate as much as I could.

Stephanie had fed Lorelai a bottle while we were at the hospital, and now she was dressed in the kind of pajamas that look like a potato sack. They are designed to make it easier to change a diaper. Everything was designed to be so simple and easy, but it was still so hard. I opened the prescription bottle of Xanax I picked up that afternoon to help with my insomnia. I took half of a tablet and then brushed my teeth. Lorelai was asleep on Noah's shoulder. He looked so calm and happy. So did she. I laid down in my bed, and for the first time since my labor was induced, my body stopped shaking and finally, blissfully, I fell into a deep sleep.

CHAPTER 10
Grandma Hardwick

At 3:00 a.m. on April 17th, I woke up for the "second shift" of Lorelai's feedings. Noah had put her to bed the night before and gave her a bottle around midnight. I had slept five hours straight, and it was incredible. It was one of those deep sleeps that left me craving more. I had a taste of rest, and it was delicious. I listlessly mixed four ounces of formula before getting Lorelai up and changed into a dry diaper. It felt like she went through a thousand diapers a day. She fell back asleep after only eating two ounces, and I found it very annoying. Eating and sleeping were Lorelai's only responsibilities, and I didn't understand why she couldn't do them separately. I still felt no attachment to her. I still looked at her with disdain. I couldn't picture a future outside of that moment.

Dark. Lonely. Tired.

I jostled her back awake and got her to down another ounce. In a couple of hours, she would turn one month old.

One month.

One month stood between me and my old life. One month was all it took for me to morph into a different being.

I didn't want to live one more hour in this endless night, and yet the moments marched on.

> "But I don't have the strength to endure.
> I have nothing to live for."
> Job 6:11 (NLT)

Imogene "Grandma" Hardwick is a petite woman in her late 70s who has had a hard life but shows no evidence of it. She laughs easily, and she cries easily. She takes in the world with wide open arms and then offers the best of it back to others with open hands. Her eyes show wisdom, and her mouth speaks kindness. She will not simply walk, but will dance, clap, jump, and giggle as she enters the gates of heaven. She had driven from her country home in Waverly, Tennessee to Ohio to meet her great-granddaughter.

She arrived early that morning, and I could hear her coming up the stairs to our apartment. Noah was with her, and he told her to take a rest at each landing but she couldn't stop talking long enough to catch her breath or stand still.

"Oh, my word, how does Lisa walk up and down all these stairs?" she asked with her sweet country accent. "Oh, honey it's so good to see you! Oh, I love you so much, oh my goodness! I just can't even believe it. Can you believe it? I am so excited. You look so good honey, I have just missed you!"

When Noah opened our door, I saw that her eyes were already full of happy tears. I sat on the couch and held a sleepy Lorelai in my arm. She burst out, "Oh, honey! She is just perfect! I can't even believe it!"

She was speechless. She just looked and gasped and cried and put her hand over her heart. She mouthed the words *she's so beautiful*. She sat to my left on the couch. We put one of the breastfeeding pillows around her lap, and then laid Lorelai on the pillow with her eyes up towards her great-grandmother. It was like Grandma Hardwick had waited her whole life to meet this child.

She was so happy. Then she looked at me, and she asked how I was feeling. She has the kind of eye contact that reads my thoughts before I can even put words together to answer. A list of automatic responses came to mind: *I'm good. I'm fine. Things are good. Things are fine. Everything is fine. It's all fine.*

"I am hopeless," I responded. I was surprised by my own impulsive honesty. Then tears. Each day of the last month passed through my memory like a recurring nightmare. I couldn't explain why I needed to cry. I couldn't explain what was wrong, and I certainly didn't know how to ask for help. She put her arm over me and let me rest on her shoulder. Lorelai slept on her lap, blissfully unaware.

"Baby, listen to me now," she said with authority. "It's going to be O.K.! Listen! We are God's children. We've got God on our side! Hallelujah! Woohoo! Thank you, Jesus! Oh, He is just so good to us, honey." She smiled because she could see the hope of my future even though she knew I was yet blind to it.

We sat together there for two hours. We were anchored to the couch by the eight-pound sleeping baby on her lap. I received a text from Stephanie that she was coming over with some groceries to "kick this sickness in the butt." She knew that wellness cannot be bought in a prescription bottle. She arrived with a trunk full of groceries and a brand-new blender. She filled our fridge with kombucha, kefir, greens, and fruit. She explained that my body is created to be strong, to survive. She decided that this sickness needed to go now, and she was going to shove it out the door herself.

The blender whirred and crushed heaps of greens and fruits and oils. A brown banana, a ripe avocado, and a scoop of yogurt were added and blended until a beautiful dark pink poured out into a big glass. I looked around the room. Grandma Hardwick smiled at me and rocked Lorelai, who appeared to be at the peak of blissful relaxation. To my right, Stephanie was now overhauling the refrigerator to restore a sense of health and home. This moment was important, but I couldn't figure out why. There was a sudden calm in my mind. It didn't necessarily make me "happy." It didn't make me smile or laugh. It didn't restore the hope I had lost, but something about being in the presence of other women who have overcome trauma and loss with such gracious strength pricked my curiosity.

How did they do it?

How did they survive the relentless torrents of this sea?

Where did their strength come from?

. . .

"Now honey, I gotta tell you something, and I don't know if you want to hear it."

Uh, oh.

That Tuesday evening Noah, Lorelai, Grandma Hardwick and me sat in a brown booth at *El Rancho Nuevo* to celebrate Lorelai's first month's birthday. It was my first opportunity to go out to eat since giving birth, and it was difficult. I had no appetite. I was nervous that we sat too far away from the toilet. I knew if I let myself eat an actual meal it would be three or more runs to the bathroom within the next half hour. I ordered a bland option and picked at my food in nausea.

Grandma Hardwick and I had passed that day together, catching up from the past few years and talking through my current situation. Postpartum depression. Postpartum anxiety. Weeks of diarrhea day and night. Insomnia. Uncontrollable weight loss. Detachment from Lorelai. The pain and the darkness. She now sat across from me, nibbling on warm tortilla chips.

"Have you asked God to heal you, honey?" she asked, turning her gaze to zero in on me.

"Yes. Of course," I responded, surprised by what appeared to be an obvious question.

"Now, honey I gotta tell you something, and I don't know if you want to hear it," she started. "You have asked God to heal you, but have you thanked Him for already healing you? He tells us we can bring Him any cares, to come to him *'by prayer and supplication with thanksgiving.'* Even when we don't see it, we can thank Him for answering because we know He listens! Honey, I know it's hard, but *we need to thank Him for our suffering.*" (Philippians 4:6)

She was right; I did not want to hear that. I didn't feel healed or hopeful or anything which would naturally bring forth a sense of thanksgiving. In fact, it made me irritated that she would ask me to thank God for this living nightmare. I replied politely and hoped to be able to put her words out of my head. I ate my food and ran to the bathroom twice. I wanted to go home. That night I slept a couple hours, and by the following morning I was still not feeling particularly thankful. I gave Lorelai her bottle then went to shower to let the hot water drown out the rest of the world for at least a few minutes.

"Be thankful. Be thankful. Be thankful," I heard in my Spirit.

"No thank you, No thank you, NO THANK YOU." I thought. Angry.

I picked up a shampoo bottle and threw it against the tile wall, satisfied by the force. I could feel myself physically fighting the words that were bubbling up in my Spirit. Then, the words were slowly spilling from my mouth. I was powerless in the presence of *His* power:

"Thank you. For the pregnancy. Thank you…thank you for the induction…thank you for the hard labor…"

In that moment of thanksgiving, nothing changed physically. However, I sensed the Lord opening my eyes to the future beyond today. Scales were ripped off. I saw beyond 2018 and beyond my own small world. My misery and my misgivings. A broader vision lay before me, and I was full of true thanks. The Lord opened my eyes to His promise.

I continued.

"Thank you…for the infection."

For in it I showed you My strength.

"Thank you for the depression."

Through it, you will bring others joy.

Tears began to flow freely. They were unlike the tears I had become accustomed to over the past month. They were not the bitter tears of disappointment and exhaustion that flowed and dried into layers of salt-caked isolation. They were tears of healing.

"Thank you for the diarrhea."

In this, you have learned humility.

"Thank you for the insomnia."

Through it, you have learned to trust in me.

"Thank you for the anxiety."

Now you can know true peace.

"Thank you for Lorelai."

She is My gift to you.

Everything changed, and yet nothing changed. There was no physical relief or miraculous surge of energy. I didn't want to jump or dance or laugh, but I knew I was healed. I realized that the brokenness of my body had brought the true healing to my soul. My eyes were opened.

"Honey," Grandma Hardwick said with a startled expression when she saw me walk out of the apartment with Lorelai in her car seat. "What happened? Something happened, didn't it? You look like…a different person. You look good, honey. Your countenance has changed."

"Everything has changed," I replied. "You were right. I just needed to thank God."

We drove ten minutes down I-75 to visit Noah at work, and I relayed the story of my revolutionary shower to her. She was ecstatic, as only Grandma Hardwick can be. She praised God, and she cried her usual happy tears.

"Honey, I gotta tell you," she said. "The day before I left to come here, I was praying to God, and He told me something. I'm serious honey, now, I wouldn't tell you no lies. He said this trip wasn't going to be about meeting my great granddaughter. That's what I thought it was for, to meet Lorelai. He told me I was going on a trip for something else. For someone else. I knew it was something urgent, and now I know I came here because of you."

CHAPTER 11
Lies

April 20th, 2018 was a very difficult day.

Our air conditioner broke again the night before, and I couldn't fall asleep. The longer I couldn't sleep, the harder it was to calm down. I couldn't calm down, so I couldn't sleep. And I couldn't sleep because I couldn't calm down. I was a hot mess. Like a veil over my eyes, the sleep deprivation and high anxiety clouded any view of reason or logic as I started the day. I became irrational, and I couldn't see past my current circumstances. Everything became an absolute. I will *never* be able to sleep again. Lorelai will *always* be a stranger. Bonding will *never* happen. My body could *never* recover from this. I will *always* feel this hopeless.

Every part of the day was a fight. From the first cries of the morning, the dashes to the bathroom, to the mind-numbing depression, I was drowning. I spoke the Scripture from Philippians 4:13: "*I can do all things through Christ who strengthens me, I can do all things through Christ who strengthens me, I can do all things…*" That statement of strength was my inner preamble as I started each day, but the weight of the world and the lies from the enemy wore me down. The baby cried and the dog barked and my ears rang. It was so loud. Yet quietly,

"*Take all the pills in the medicine cabinet. You can make it all go away.*"

The Good Shepherd was not the speaker. I knew it wasn't His voice, but it sounded so appealing. I was weak. Physically. Emotionally. I knew I had enough medication in the cabinet to kill myself. It seemed like a practical solution to the pain. Logical thought went out the window. The depression became too much. The lies began to repeat, like a record player turning quietly but steadily in the background. Irrational thoughts became rational as the record whined on,

"Take all the pills in the medicine cabinet. You know there is enough to stop your heart. It will be easy. Lorelai won't even remember it. She can have a better mother. Just do it. Do it."

Although I had entertained a few suicidal thoughts as my postpartum depression developed, this time the option to kill myself seemed so tangible. So comforting. I knew that these lies were from the enemy, but my broken mind couldn't see beyond this one moment. It was a temporary situation that appeared eternal. I wanted the pain to stop. Forever. I wanted the terror to leave my mind. I would do anything to escape my body.

"Go! Get out! Anywhere! Go, Lisa, Go!" the Shepherd called.

It was a rush for the door. I packed a bag and the baby, and we got out of the apartment and into the car. I took a breath. I had a key to my in-law's house, and I texted Stephanie that we were going to stop by so Lorelai and I could have a change of scenery. It was a Friday, and there was a chance she worked from home. Regardless, I knew it would be a safe place. I drove the familiar route to my in-law's house. I had pulled into this same driveway hundreds of times. It felt like home. I could see Stephanie in the kitchen as I sat in the car. I knew God planned for her to work from home that day. I knew I made the right decision to leave our apartment, although it didn't take any of the pain away. I did not want to live. I saw no reason for it.

"I'm just having a hard time," were the only words I could say before I melted into tears. I told her about the lies from the enemy that I couldn't fight by myself. I told her I had nothing left. "I can't keep going."

She let me cry on her shoulder. Lorelai slept in her car seat on the floor.

"Oh, yes you can do this," she told me with a confidence I knew I could believe in. "Yes, you can. You can and you will. You don't have any other choice. You're exhausted. You just gave birth. You are vulnerable right now. Never forget we are all in this together. It's not just you fighting, we are all with you." She handed me a cup of coffee and we sat on the couch.

She asked me if I could breathe. I told her I could. She told me to take another breath. I did. She said that is how I would survive the hardest moments. I had to sit in the reality of the chaos, breathe, and wait for the stress to wash over me. Like a tidal wave at the beach, the moment would soon end. Then I would breathe in another moment. I could no longer think about the next two million moments I would face in the future or what those moments would look like. I only had to survive one at a time. One moment at a time. One breath at a time.

It sounded doable.

We talked through my fears. She spoke the truth to me. Over and over and over again until I began to believe it. *Yes, you can. You can and you will. Yes, you can. You can and you will.* We got through the next hour. I gave Lorelai a bottle while I watched Netflix. I sipped on a bottle of strawberry kefir, but I still found myself with diarrhea about every half-hour. It just wouldn't stop. The sun came out, and I pushed Lorelai in her stroller. I took the familiar half-mile loop, and she cried the whole time. It was worth it to feel the warmth of spring. We got through another hour.

Stephanie made me a plate of food, but I couldn't eat. I finished the bottle of kefir and watched more T.V. I gave Lorelai her bottle, and we got through another hour. And another. Each one felt like a tiny eternity.

At 4:00 that afternoon, I headed home. I couldn't stop thinking about suicide. I wanted to go to heaven. I wanted Lorelai to have a better mother. Someone who loves her and wants her. Someone other than me. I couldn't do another day of this. I knew the enemy was working overtime to try and convince me of these lies. Why else would death seem so appealing? I drove past Keehner Park. Everything was green. I thought about the times Noah and I hiked through their familiar dirt trails that wind in and out of the woods at the back of the park. I wanted to go back in time when it was just the two of us. But I couldn't. I thought about how devastated Noah would be if I killed myself. The initial shock would break him into a million pieces. He would have to live in mourning and unanswered questions.

I could not do that to him.

To me? Could I cut my life short and forfeit any chance for hope? Could I be a coward and take the back door out of life? Yes.

To Lorelai? Could I take away the person she knew the best? Could I leave her without a mother? Yes.

But for Noah? No.

I did not want to hurt him. I wanted to give him his wife back.

I felt suffocated when I returned to our apartment. It was the same. Same pile of laundry. Same baby bottles in the sink. Same spilled powder next to the same expensive tub of infant formula. The baby cried and the dog barked. Nothing had changed. I was still drowning and hadn't slept in the last 40 hours. Stress hormones sent familiar shock waves through my body and left my ears buzzing.

At 5:00 p.m. Heather knocked on the door. She had signed up to bring us a meal that day. Barbecued chicken, cornbread, green beans and four huge cupcakes, each one a different flavor with a generous pouf of icing. I still had no appetite, and just the thought of food sent me to the bathroom in pain. I explained to her that my stomach was still volatile. She asked me how I was doing, and I answered her honestly. I was not doing well. Not at all. Heather was a friend from our church who also volunteered with the high school ministry. She had mentored dozens of high school girls over the past years, and she had learned to be a patient listener. I told her that I knew the enemy kept telling me lies to commit suicide.

"You realize this is not Lisa talking, right?" she asked me. "This is not you. I know you, and this is definitely not you. Don't believe the lies. You have to believe in the Truth."

Noah came home from work soon after Heather left, and our family made it through another day. One more day, one more victory. One single moment at a time.

CHAPTER 12
The Doctors

I arrived at my appointment with Lorelai strapped to me in her carrier. We called it her *papoose*. It was gray with a white fleur-de-lis design that camouflaged spit-up stains surprisingly well. I sat in the psychiatric department's waiting room and checked off boxes and boxes of symptoms. Down the hallway, I could see the obstetric department's waiting area and immediately across the hall sat a handful of pregnant women waiting next to the door marked "Imaging." This was the women's department. It was painted the same lilac hue as the Labor and Delivery department in the hospital across the street. Muted canvas prints with simple nature scenes hung from the walls and calm music played to soothe the environment. Anything could happen here. Just try to stay calm.

"It's a girl!"
"It's a boy!"
"Twins!"
"The test is negative."
"The test is positive."
"I can't find the heartbeat."

Motherhood in its nature is wildly unpredictable and profoundly emotional.

That's why I sat in front of the door that read "Psychiatrics."

The nurse recorded my blood pressure and pulse. Lorelai fell asleep in her papoose as I swayed back and forth. I met Dr. S., who wore a black pant suit and black heels and had a tidy white bookcase. She handed me a clipboard with the Edinburgh Postnatal Depression Scale. I had grown familiar with this test and circled my answers with a ballpoint pen. Dr. S told me I once again scored a 29/30 which was, in her opinion, "very bad." She took off her glasses and held my eye contact. She seemed to study me for a moment, and then asked about my history with mental health. And Lorelai's birth. And my living situation. And my childhood. And every other detail she could cover over the next forty-five minutes.

I wasn't just another patient. I was me, and I needed help.

She told me I made the right decision to stop breastfeeding. I couldn't believe it. What about all the health benefits of breastmilk? What about the posters and the public service announcements? She told me I couldn't take care of my baby if I didn't take care of myself. It seemed like a simple enough concept, but one that I struggled to accept. We talked about my history with an eating disorder. I had to pull out details I had buried away so long ago. She then asked me to remember back and think about what the recovery process looked like.

"What did it take to recover?" she asked.

"Work." I replied. I knew it was the right answer.

"Correct. You have to work."

She agreed my situation was very difficult, but she said it would improve. She increased the prescription for Zoloft and prescribed 30 doses of Xanax to take for the next month to get my body back to regular sleep cycles. I was sleeping three to four hours in a twenty-four-hour period, and she said I needed more. Lorelai was five weeks old and was already dominating five-hour stretches of deep sleep at night. She knew how to sleep, and I was the one who had a hard time. The diarrhea had improved a little each day. I was down to five or six times a day, which was much better than round the clock life in the bathroom. I had an appetite again. The worst was over.

She assigned me to a support group for patients with severe perinatal mental health illnesses. The group met every Tuesday at 10:00 a.m. in the conference room down the hallway. The psychologist of the women's center would oversee each meeting and guide discussions. The group accommodated patients who were pregnant or up to twenty-four months postpartum. Dr. S told me that prescription medication alone is unable to treat an illness. It would take work and healthy lifestyle habits to bring complete wellness. It would take a support structure and outside help. It would be a process, but it was possible.

We set up a plan for how to survive the next couple weeks. She told me to continue to build my support structure, to remind myself I was not alone. She told me it was best if Noah continued to feed Lorelai during the night. She told me I needed to take my medicine every day. She told me to keep eating as much as I could, to meditate when I couldn't sleep, and to be outside as much as possible. She explained how to breathe deep when everything blurred into panic mode. She reminded me I did the right thing to switch to formula. She told me to write and write and write.

There is something about writing that heals the hurt.

Lorelai squirmed and whined in her papoose as the appointment came to an end. I set up an appointment to return in two weeks. I felt hopeful. I rushed home and gave Lorelai a bottle. I didn't want to be with her, and I didn't know why. Logically, I knew she was a wonderful baby, but the bond was just not there.

We survived another day. She cried, and I cried. She slept and I cleaned the kitchen again. I stared out the window and prayed this could all be a bad dream.

* * *

"I hear you say the words 'worried' and 'anxious' but let's call it what it is. Fear. What are you afraid of?"

Dr. Jean leaned back and gave me time to find an answer. It was a Tuesday at 10:10 a.m., and we sat around a conference table on the fourth floor. The sun pooled through a wall of windows. Lorelai was tucked in her papoose as I rocked in my swivel chair. She was almost two months old and nodded in and out of consciousness as the conversation went on. It was my first meeting at the perinatal support group that Dr. S. assigned me to. I was the only patient that day. Me and Dr. Jean.

"I don't know," I mused. "The future. The unknown. I have always hated the unknown."

"So, is it just an underlying sense of dread?" she asked.

"Yes! Exactly. I can't explain why, but it won't stop. I can't turn my brain off, especially at night." Tears found their familiar pool in my eyes and down my cheeks which felt hot and hollow.

I was too embarrassed to mention the nightly self-medication I had implemented in the last week. In desperation to fall asleep, I washed down a cocktail of extra-strength Tylenol, melatonin, Unisom, and Benadryl with a beer. Since I had stopped breastfeeding, I could see no reason not to drink. It lessened that *underlying sense of dread* for at least a few minutes.

"Worrying about the future makes no difference. It doesn't change anything. Do you know that?" she asked.

"I do. Yes. In my head I know, but I just can't stop thinking about it," I tried to explain to her what I could not explain to myself. "I just can't slow down my brain."

She explained that when I worry about the future, I take away the joy of the present. When I begin to panic about the *what-ifs*, I have to learn to force myself back to the present moment. Dr. Jean said that fear is a good and appropriate emotion if my life is in danger. Other than that, it's not necessary. I needed to ask myself the question, *"How am I now? Right now, in this moment, is my life in danger?"* If my life was not in danger, then I needed to identify the source of the fear. What am I afraid of?

"I'm afraid of getting sick again and having to go back to the hospital," I told her. "I'm afraid of getting pregnant. I'm afraid of Lorelai getting sick like me. I'm afraid of the nights. I'm afraid we can't afford a child."

Dr. Jean nodded and smiled. "Good. Now we have identified the real fear."

When I began to identify a specific fear instead of being overcome with a general feeling of anxiety, I was able to see my life in a different light. I was not being attacked or threatened by any true source, but my thoughts had gotten so far out of control that I was living in a constant state of panic. I was not living in reality. The goal was not to change my *circumstances*, but to change my *thoughts* about the circumstances.

"There is a difference between preparation and worry," Dr. Jean explained.

I could continue to spend my time in my own head and worry about future sicknesses. I could think about all the very real illnesses and pain that exist throughout the world. I could stay awake all night and sit in fear of all the worst-case scenarios in every situation of my life. I could develop ulcers and high blood pressure out of the what-ifs. I could worry all I wanted, but it wouldn't change a thing. Instead, I needed to learn how to take care of my body to prepare it for the future. I could have a healthy lifestyle and rest in the fact that I did the best I could do *today*. If my life is not in danger, right *now*, there's no need for fear.

> "So, don't worry about these things, saying, 'What will we eat? What will we drink? What will we wear?' These things dominate the thoughts of unbelievers, but your heavenly father already knows all your needs. Seek the Kingdom of God above all else, and live righteously, and he will give you everything you need. So, don't worry about tomorrow, for tomorrow will bring its own worries. Today's trouble is enough for today."
> Matthew 6:31-34 (NLT)

I started to put tools in my toolbox. These mental health professionals were not here to medicate me and send me out the door. They wanted to give me the right tools to manage my symptoms. They were on my team. They were on Lorelai's team. They wanted us to thrive together. Long-term. It wasn't only about the prescriptions or the dosages. It was about a lifestyle change.

At first, I thought I was one of a few select women who found themselves with such wild behaviors and thought patterns after giving birth. No. I was one of millions. How many of those millions thought they, too, were the only ones to experience postpartum depression? How many women had kept their secrets buried out of fear? How many women had to suffer in silence? What I came to realize is this:

Too many.

Way too many.

Too many women are left to sit in darkness and grow unwarranted guilt like a garden. Too many women believe the lie that they are a burden if they speak up to ask for help. Too many fear judgement from their family. Friends. Society. The longer they sit in darkness, the deeper their symptoms and thought patterns ingrain into daily life. Sleep deprivation is mixed with raging hormonal surges, and they can't think straight. They don't know how to ask for help. Their bodies are torn open after nine months of building a human, and then they are expected to nurse these precious pink babies that cry and throw up and poop and never ever say "thank you." Many of these women have other tiny humans in the mix whose endless needs do not diminish just because a new sibling has made an appearance.

How many women were buried under depression?

Too many. I knew it was too many.

CHAPTER 13
New Moms

By two months postpartum, things looked brighter. The Zoloft began to kick in, and my prescription was increased from 100 mg to 150 mg. I still cried every day, but I could get through conversations without breaking down. I could eat again, and my stomach continued to heal itself. My day-to-day life was no longer dominated by diarrhea. I swallowed my probiotics and drank those green smoothies. I tried to take a walk every day. I was able to take a deep breath every once in a while. I still had no desire to be with Lorelai. I couldn't accept the thought that she was mine.

Despite this notable progress, I began to drink every night. I was afraid of the sleepless hours and the quiet time in the middle of the night when everything was dark and everyone was asleep but me. Lorelai was on a sleep schedule and impressed me with her consistency. It was like she had learned how to sleep while I forgot. My body couldn't seem to remember how to shut itself down.

I was desperate for sleep.

I had severe joint pain in my elbows, wrists, and fingers. I wasn't used to holding a baby all the time, and my shoulders were screaming at me. The pain built over the first two months of handling a newborn. One Sunday afternoon, my right shoulder locked up, and I couldn't lift my arm without searing pain. It was scary. Noah was able to help keep things moving, but I felt so broken.

By mid-June, Tulip developed a row of bumps on her back. We thought it was an allergic reaction to a flea and tick medication we put on her skin. She was nine years old, and she did not want to share any attention with Lorelai. She had been our "only child" furbaby for almost a decade before Lorelai showed up, and she began to act depressed. She followed me everywhere, which included getting up and down and up and down from the bed at night during the first weeks postpartum. She never showed any aggression towards Lorelai, but she did appear confused, hurt, and unsure of herself. It broke my heart.

We gave her a bath and assumed her bumps would calm down after a few days.

I began to attend "park play dates" with the Mom's Group of our church. Even though Lorelai wasn't able to play, I was still invited to come sit in the sun and enjoy adult conversation. I felt like a stunned animal among veteran mothers. I still couldn't manage to talk about my labor and delivery without panic or tears. I didn't talk much at all, but I was grateful for the company and the sunshine.

For twelve weeks, I spent every Tuesday from 10:00 a.m. to 10:55 a.m. in the conference room on the fourth floor of the medical building. I normally brought Lorelai with me. I pushed her stroller into the bright conference room with the glass windows and the swivel chairs. Lorelai fussed and whined, as babies do. I mixed a bottle of formula for her while other patients arrived. There were four other group members who showed up on a consistent basis. We all had Dr. S as our psychiatrist, and we were all instructed to commit to twelve weeks of the program.

We were the patients who got really high scores on the postpartum depression screening tests. Straight-A students.

I met Crystal the second week of the support group. She had discovered her surprise pregnancy as a newlywed in Chicago. She had recently begun a prestigious residency program to earn her M.D., but then morning sickness began. Then it turned into all-day sickness. She fell behind and lost her residency position. Without an income stream, the couple couldn't keep up financially and declared bankruptcy. They moved in with her parents in Ohio when she was in her third trimester. She had planned to complete her residency and pursue practice as a family medicine doctor. Instead, she was back in her high school bedroom with her new husband and a fussy baby.

It was just too much.

Nancy had a 20-month old son, and she was pregnant with her second child. She was 43 years old, and both pregnancies were surprises. In fact, Nancy's husband got a vasectomy after the birth of their son. God had different plans. She was just coming up from the darkness of the postpartum depression with her first child when she saw yet another surprise plus sign on a pregnancy test. She was angry and she was scared. Nancy and her husband were married seventeen years before having children. The reality of raising two tiny humans demolished their dreams of early retirement to enjoy the quiet life they had built for themselves. After a month of these meetings, she confessed she wanted to take all of the insulin that was available for her gestational diabetes in order to kill herself and the fetus. She checked herself into a psychiatric in-patient program.

It was just too much.

Dawn suffered from bipolar disorder, and her son was 5 months old. She lived with her boyfriend and his parents who spoke little English. She spent days at a time in the darkness of her bedroom during episodes of deep depression. When she experienced a manic episode, she couldn't stop herself from maxing out credit cards and binge drinking herself into a stupor. She struggled through medication changes as the psychiatrist tried various combinations of prescriptions to minimize the extreme peaks and valleys. She also checked herself into a psychiatric ward after auditory and visual hallucinations became indistinguishable from her reality and she could no longer care for her son.

It was just too much.

Tiffany was a young, fashionable professional who lived with her boyfriend in a small house in the trendy part of Cincinnati. They hadn't planned to have a baby, but she soon fell in love with those tiny fingers and toes. She adored her 6-month-old daughter, but she couldn't sleep at night. Or eat enough. She couldn't sit still. I recognized that as anxiety. She battled thoughts of suicide, and she wouldn't let anyone but her husband or her mother hold the baby. She cried often, and she couldn't focus. I knew that was the depression. She knew she loved her baby, but she also knew something was wrong. She had lost herself, and she didn't know how to function in this new life as a mother.

It was just too much.

Each meeting began with a check-in. Each patient was required to give a synopsis of their prior week. It was healing to hear everyone else's struggles. It reminded me I was not alone. Dr. Jean never looked shocked or surprised by anyone's confessions. She nodded and leaned back in her chair. She didn't take notes or give opinions during our check-ins, but she always told each patient, "thank you for sharing." It became the place we knew we could say anything without receiving judgement or blame. She set the example, and we learned from each other's vulnerabilities.

After a few weeks of the support group, a close family member had a baby of her own. A son, her first child. She and I had talked about the future while both of our bumps continued to grow during the previous months of pregnancy. We both wanted to pursue a natural birth, with no pain medication or medical intervention. We both wanted to breastfeed for a year. At least. She worked in a daycare for several years and had already won the gold medal on diaper-changing technique. Her labor was induced, but she gave birth with no pain medicine. She did what I had wanted to do. She refused Pitocin and stuck it out. She was decisive and confident in her choices, and it paid off.

I felt like such a failure.

I hadn't reached my goal of a natural birth, which I had held on a pedestal in my mind. I wanted to tell everyone I was able to tough it out too. No one was disappointed in me. No one, but me.

Lorelai cried while we drove to the hospital to meet the newest member of our family. It was loud. I could feel the anxiety twist around my chest. She continued her wails as we arranged her in the stroller and walked through the revolving doors into the hospital lobby. I couldn't take a decent breath by the time we reached the maternity ward. Machines beeped and buzzed and nurses scurried from one patient to the next with their scrubs and their stethoscopes. I wanted to leave. I didn't want to be in any hospital. I was afraid, but I couldn't explain why.

This is where terrible things happen, I thought. *This is the place where all the pain begins.*

We strolled down to the end of the hallway where our family was gathered around the new mom and the little baby swaddled in a soft gray blanket. She had her curly hair brushed into a ponytail and wore a headband to keep the wandering wisps out of her eyes. She wore thick black glasses and her cheeks were rosy pink. She looked so natural as a mom, as if she had waited her whole life for this very moment. I saw her tired eyes, but her mouth smiled with contentment. The baby was perfect. His head was covered with thick, dark hair and his skin was flawlessly smooth and soft.

Lorelai cried, and Stephanie rescued her from her stroller. Both babies were passed around and admired and given lots of "oohs" and "ahhs." When no one was able to calm Lorelai down from her cries, I held her the way I knew she liked. On her stomach, where she could look around and see everything that was happening. She didn't want to be held on her back where she could only see the ceiling or the face of the person who held her. She always wanted to be in the know. We spoke briefly with the new parents, and Noah prayed for the new baby while we all held hands. Everyone seemed so happy. It was a beautiful moment, but I was overcome with sadness.

I cried the whole drive home. I couldn't explain why. It just hurt.

> "But each one must carefully scrutinize his own work [examining his actions, attitudes, and behaviors], and then he can have the personal satisfaction and inner joy of doing something commendable without comparing himself to another."
> *Galatians 6:4 (AMP)*

I thought I was doing really well. I thought I was on the path up and out of depression and that I could continue to walk the even incline towards freedom and light and life. I told myself that every day would be a tiny bit better than the day before. Each week would be an improvement from the prior week. The weeks would build into months, and I could look forward to improved mental and physical health with each new month. Surely it would be over soon.

When I began to compare myself with other new mothers, I fell off the wagon. The progress stopped. It made me angry that other women didn't have to suffer like this. I witnessed my own family member and her new baby bond together like peanut butter and jelly stuck between two pieces of warm toast. They seemed so in sync. I knew logically that I loved Lorelai. Otherwise I wouldn't have worked so hard to keep her alive for this long. She was always clean, fed, dressed, and safe. But I was afraid to be around her. Or I grew resentful with her ceaseless cries and endless needs. I had nothing left to give, but she continued to demand. I began to think something was wrong with me. Really wrong. *Why didn't I want to be around my own baby? When would we finally bond? Would we ever bond? Would I always resent her?*

I told myself I failed at labor because I used pain medicine. I failed at breastfeeding because I stopped so soon. I failed as a wife because I didn't live up to the expectations I *thought* were appropriate for a stay-at-home mom. I failed as a mom, because I couldn't look my daughter in the eyes and say, "I love you." I was drowning in self-condemnation because of some unspoken rules and idealistic expectations that the world created and I adopted. I perceived perfection to be the goal, and anything less than that was a glaring failure for all to see.

I didn't want to "do the work" anymore to build a healthy mental state. I was tired of doing the work, and I didn't see anyone else doing it. The progress I had made over the past two months seemed worthless. The road ahead now looked too hard and too steep, and I was not strong enough. I was not meant for this. I made a mistake. I made a bad decision. I wanted out, and I wanted out now. I could not put one foot in front of the other. I could not get out of bed every morning and live this life. I couldn't do it.

I gave up.

"So I gave up in despair,
questioning the value of all my hard work in the world."

Ecclesiastes 2:20 (NLT)

CHAPTER 14
June Journals

I started to write more, since I was told it would help me heal. These journal entries from June 2018 best display my experience from that time.

JUNE 12:
I don't feel like trying anymore – I feel like the battle is still going, but I've bled out from the wounds I've been dealt the last 3 months. "Just be still and the Lord will fight your battles," but I feel alone on the battlefield. I'm sorry, Lord, for my disbelief. Forgive me for my fear. I feel guilty for feeling this way. I want to just take the easy way out, sneaking out the back door of life without bravely moving forward. But I couldn't hurt Noah in that way. I don't care enough about Lorelai and if it were just she and I, I would check out. But Noah, I love. I can't do that to him, he would be forever devastated. I feel lonely but I know it's not true, it's just Satan trying to isolate me.

    I fear I'll never feel good again in my body. I fear I'll never have a good night's sleep. I can't even fall asleep without a lot of medication. Other people enjoy sleep but I fear trying to sleep & failing like I did so much in March and April. I worry my daughter will have a weird personality because of me. Will she be under-socialized because I can only handle one child and we want to homeschool? I'm afraid people will judge me and think I'm doing her a disservice. I fear Noah wants his old wife back. I fear he can't put up with me.

Do I want to be healed? Or do I want to lean on the identity of depression? It's comfortable to me. I know it. Jesus, Jesus, Jesus, I am falling short. Will you still love me? Are you annoyed by me? I keep repeating the same patterns. I'm sorry, Lord. Forgive me, I'm sorry.

• • •

JUNE 13:
Feeling a wee bit better today! The Lord has restored a sense of Joy in me. I feel like I'm a disappointment if all I do is self-care and domestic activities. Like I'm lazy. Maybe this is just how this particular season can look. Sometimes I look at Lorelai and I just think, *"How beautiful and special she is!"* But it's followed up with complete sadness. Like a brick falling on my heart.

Lord, I pray you would fill my heart with not only love, but enjoyment for Lorelai as well as for my role as *mom*.

Dad, I feel like I'm just so needy. I feel like I just ask, ask, ask and then I neglect You when it's not convenient.

JUNE 14:
The last three days have been dominated by suicidal thoughts. Woke up and felt like I was in a trance. Kept hearing the repetitive message to kill myself. Like a tape recorder over and over.

JUNE 17:
Last night I opened my wrist and forearm with my nails and a nail clipper. That was low, but I feel a relief from the pain of life via the physical pain. I feel embarrassed. I cried most of the day yesterday. I am feeling defeated. Noah reminds me I am victorious. Today is Father's Day. Earlier this week I thought, *"I couldn't kill myself*

right before Father's Day." Noah says to tell the lies NO and to back it up with Scripture. I just feel like the Lord is far away, even though Scriptures say that He is near. What is wrong with me?

Lorelai is a good baby and she sleeps a lot, but I'm still so exhausted and drained. This day is a challenging day in my faith. I will write down things I KNOW are truth, but don't FEEL like truth right now.

1. Lorelai is a gift from God.
2. Hope is a byproduct of the Spirit.
3. God loves me.
4. God will never leave me, nor forsake me.
5. God will work all things together for my good.
6. I will run and not grow weary.
7. The Kingdom is here on earth now.
8. I am victorious through Jesus Christ.

Daddy Daddy Abba Dad — my spirit is willing, but my flesh is SO WEAK. I am unable to maintain *"a sound mind."* Why have you abandoned me? When will I find relief? I plead the blood of Jesus Christ over my mind — I plead the power of Jesus' death and resurrection over my life. Holy Spirit, come. Holy Spirit, reign.

JUNE 20:
I felt a sense of relief these last couple days. Like I'm back on my feet even if my legs are wobbly.

JUNE 28:
On Sunday, the message at church was about depression. I went up to the front and was prayed over for healing and anointed with oil. Jesus, precious and merciful savior. The man who withstood all my transgressions. Jesus, I pray for physical healing from this disease. Just a touch of the hem of your garment sweet Lord. I heard the Lord say to surrender the control. Teach me how Lord.

I am afraid. Because I want to know all things, but only you know all things. I already don't have any control. It's just an allusion. I fear the unexpected but I have to believe it will all be for His glory and for my good. How do you give up something (ex: CONTROL) that you don't even have? It's like a placebo or something. Jesus help me I don't know — my spirit is willing but my flesh is so weak.

JULY 13

Today was the first day I enjoyed my child and had moments of enjoying motherhood.

CHAPTER 15

July

July was good. Lots of good things happened.

On July 4th, my best friend from Nashville drove up to stay with us for a few days. Then the air conditioner went out again, and it was hot. That night my friend and I danced in the grass with sparklers and party hats and she taught me how to laugh again. It felt really good to laugh. July 19th was our 10-year wedding anniversary. We stuck with tradition and made pancakes for dinner. I could exercise again, and I was proud of my body for surviving the last few months. I began to treat it with a respect I didn't have before. I was impressed that it had overcome so much.

July was hard. Lots of difficult things happened.

Routine blood work showed that Noah carried the Hashimoto gene, which had put his thyroid in a sad state. We had to alter his diet and begin a supplement regimen to try and heal his body. It was expensive. Tulip's skin condition worsened, and the vet couldn't pinpoint the origin of what looked like painful sores on her back. We also had to alter her diet and begin a regimen of antibiotics. It was expensive. I knew the enemy was trying to hit me where it hurt. My man, my dog, and my bank account.

The day-to-day life of any stay-at-home mom with a baby is hard. It's work, and it's endless. It was thankless.

I continued to battle suicidal thoughts. At four months postpartum, I was still deeply depressed. I felt no attachment to Lorelai. She had already grown to be smart and curious and beautiful, but I couldn't accept the reality that she was *my* daughter. I still wanted to go back to my "old life." I didn't want to be a mom. I fed her, bathed her, changed her, clothed her, and burped her like a robot. I could repeat the motions, but I put no heart in it. I just wanted it to be over. I hated to hear her cries. I couldn't drum up an ounce of empathy; I only resented her.

* * *

I was prescribed Trazodone to alleviate my insomnia, and it worked. I called it my *elephant tranquilizer*. I hated to think that my body was now reliant on a prescription medication for sleep, but I took it nonetheless. The frenzied panic that accompanies sleep deprivation waned. I could sleep for six or more hours at a time, and I could even nap when I wanted to. It was glorious. I could finally do what I had planned to do since day one as a new mother: *sleep when the baby sleeps.*

That was the plan before all the plans went out the window.

I wrote Scriptures down on scraps of paper and taped them around the apartment. If I sat on the couch, I read Psalms 61:2 that stuck to the coffee table. It gave me hope. *"From the end of the earth I call to you when my heart is faint. Lead me to the rock that is higher than I."* (ESV)

If I cooked in the kitchen, I read Joshua 1:9 because it gave me strength. *"Have I not commanded you? Be strong and courageous. Do not be frightened, and do not be dismayed, for the Lord your God is with you wherever you go."* (ESV)

Every time I washed my hands in the bathroom, I read Psalms 16:8 so I could remember where to look. *"I keep my eyes always on the Lord. With him at my right hand, I will not be shaken."* (NIV)

In my closet, I chose Psalms 118:5-6 because it reminded me how far the Lord had already taken me towards healing. *"In my distress I prayed to the Lord, and the Lord answered me and set me free. The Lord is for me, so I will have no fear. What can mere people do to me?"* (NLT)

When I changed the seven hundredth dirty diaper of the day, I had a card stuck to Lorelai's changing table that read Titus 2:4-5. I didn't particularly like the Scripture, but I needed it. It reminded me of my call to humility. *"And so train the young women to love their husbands and children, to be self-controlled, pure, working at home, kind, and submissive to their own husbands, that the word of God may not be reviled."* (ESV)

These little white pieces of scrap paper brought me security. As a human, I am forgetful and need constant reminders that God is faithful. Like a goldfish, sometimes I forget as soon as I turn around.

I joined a Bible study group with members of my church's "Mom's Group." We read through two books together and we met at Alyssa's house every Wednesday morning that summer. There were seven of us moms. Their older kids were watched by a babysitter, but Lorelai sat with me and I fed her a bottle. Then she was held by one of the other women when I inevitably needed a break. She was rocked and loved and snuggled by these other women when I needed to just have space to weep and mourn. To hug and to be hugged. To hold and to be held. We all cried a lot of tears that summer.

Every week, we brought our regrets and our shame and our fears and we laid them out in front of each other. We let go of years of secret, festering pain that we no longer allowed to dominate our minds. We tasted authenticity and we grew to crave it. We learned how to tear down our walls and leave our masks at the front door. We let it all hang out, and God healed us in ways we didn't know we needed. The Holy Spirit brought us together, and we got to see a glimpse of perfect grace. It was life-changing. We finally allowed ourselves the mercy we had been given through Jesus' suffering on the cross and we allowed others to step in and love us in our mess.

> "No one has ever seen God.
> But if we love each other, God lives in us, and his love is brought to full expression in us.
> And God has given us his Spirit as proof that we live in him and he in us."
>
> 1 John 4:12-13 (NLT)

I still had a hard time at night. I couldn't sit still. Starting at 8:00 p.m. I paced from room to room. I couldn't control my body; it just took over. I shook. My chest got tight. I cried. I became unbearably sad. Afraid. I was scared to drive anywhere or be far away from home. When we gave Lorelai a final bottle, Noah always held her with her head on his shoulder as she began her night of sleep. I just wanted to take the Trazodone and go to sleep as soon as I could. I wanted to escape. I practiced meditation once I was in bed, so that I wouldn't let my wandering thoughts get the best of me. I had to learn to concentrate on thoughts that would help me rest, not help me worry.

It took practice, but each day I could concentrate one or two seconds more than the day before. I could keep my mind from chasing rabbits down dark holes, even if it was only for a few minutes. I closed my eyes and pictured my ideal setting. Each night I envisioned a small house on the top of a mountain. Everything outside was green and peaceful. The floors were wooden, and the walls were painted teal. Flowers bloomed everywhere. On the walls, on the windowsills, hung from the ceiling and scattered in vases. Yellow, pink, and orange flowers danced on the teal walls, and I took a deep breath. Maybe that's what heaven will be like, only much better.

I inhaled for four seconds, held my breath for seven seconds, and exhaled for eight seconds. Dr. S had taught me this technique, and I could feel the weight lifting from my chest with each breath. I forced out all the stress that I had hoarded throughout the day with the long exhales. Out of my chest, out of my stomach, out of the tightness in my shoulders. Once I was able to take a deep breath, I could focus. I envisioned myself in the middle of this flower house, and all of my worries were stones in a bag I held over my shoulder. The Lord was with me, and he wanted me to hand them over. One by one I pulled a stone from my bag and wrote out each worry.

Money.

Baby.

Marriage.

One by one, I named the fear and threw it out the open window. God had it. He took it away, and I couldn't have it back. I continued this mental exercise each night until I fell asleep. It was like a bedtime prayer.

> "Give all your worries and cares to God, for he cares about you."
>
> 1 Peter 5:7 (NLT)

I prayed a lot. It was my lifeline. It became my everything. I slowed down to take life one moment at a time. I had no other option. I loved God, and I knew He was at work. In the midst of the anxiety and the monotony, I could cling to the promises of my heavenly Father. While my body changed and adjusted to new medications and hormones, I knew God was the one who created and sustained me. He hadn't let me die in my bathroom.

He didn't let me die from the infection. He had kept me alive, and I trusted that He had a reason for it. I didn't want to fight for myself. I didn't want to get better for my own sake.

I wanted to get better for the Lord. I wanted to get better for Noah. I wanted to get better for other women like me. The ones who suffered through the same tear-filled nights. I wanted to get better for the patients that I cried with on Tuesday mornings. I wanted to get better for my friends who had so much hope for me and my baby. The ones who texted and called and hugged me every day because they knew I needed them desperately. I wanted to get better for the women who brought me dinner and sat with me in my misery. I wanted to get better for the dozens of people, known and unknown, who prayed for me. For my body to heal, for my heart to heal, for the light to break through the darkness. I wanted to get better, but I didn't think it would ever actually happen.

Could I ever really, truly have a loving, healthy relationship with my daughter?

Could I ever be myself again?

Could I ever give my husband his wife back?

I just didn't believe it. But the future no longer mattered as much as it did before, so I continued to try and live one moment to the next. Moments created days and days made weeks, but I only had to think about one at a time. One breath at a time strung together with whispered prayers and a holy hope that defied the logic and reason I used to rely on. It was a beautiful renaissance. I began to find true strength in my weakness.

> "Three different times I begged the Lord to take it away.
> Each time he said,
> 'My grace is all you need. My power works best in weakness.' So now I am glad to boast about my weaknesses, so that the power of Christ can work

through me. That's why I take pleasure in my weaknesses, and in the insults, hardships, persecutions, and troubles that I suffer for Christ. For when I am weak, then I am strong."

2 Corinthians 12:8-10 (NLT)

CHAPTER 16
Vacation

I didn't know I was allowed to go on a vacation when Lorelai was only five months old. I thought it sounded too good to be true. Stephanie and Dan, Noah's mother and stepfather, offered to watch Lorelai at their house while we took a trip to celebrate our 10th wedding anniversary. A vacation? After all of this? I had grown accustomed to being a patient with a list of symptoms, not a real person who is capable of having fun and taking a trip. Would I be able to leave home for that long? What about at night? When I thought about driving, I felt a surge of anxiety. It seemed like a big giant step, but I was only used to taking baby steps.

I didn't know of many people who traveled before their child's first birthday. Nobody I knew. But since we formula fed Lorelai and she graciously slept through the night, I felt confident that she could survive and thrive in a new environment for a few days. I wrote down her feeding schedule, her nap schedule, and we did a one-night test run with his parents at the beginning of August. It was the first night I was away from Lorelai since her birth, and it was incredible. We dropped her off, and I anticipated I might cry or suddenly miss her desperately.

No.

I did not cry.

We went out and ate dinner and drank wine and played sand volleyball with our friends. We laughed and met new people, and I felt alive. I forgot how it felt to have fun. I didn't give a thought to Lorelai. I trusted that Stephanie and Dan were perfectly competent and devoted grandparents that would do their darnedest to make sure nothing happened to their granddaughter. I gave myself the opportunity to not think about her and I could sit back and relax. A friend of mine and I talked about dogs and art and how to put on liquid eyeliner without looking like a raccoon. It seemed like the most stimulating conversation I had been a part of in months. It was so simple. I loved it.

I woke up the next morning and didn't have a crying baby to feed. I didn't have a dirty diaper to change. I didn't have to wipe off a hot smear of spit up from my shirt. I drank coffee, I pet Tulip, and I read the Bible. I felt like I was on vacation already. Noah slept late, and I was glad. He needed the extra hours of uninterrupted sleep. I thought I would miss Lorelai, but I didn't. I couldn't decide if that was a bad thing or a good thing, but I just didn't. I was so thankful to have this moment to just sit. I didn't turn on the television or music. I just sat in the silence and read.

I cried on the way to pick up Lorelai. I didn't want this experience to end. I needed more time. I felt guilty that I wasn't excited to see my baby. I attributed this to the postpartum depression. I reminded myself that I was still quite sick. I would continue "to do the work" to help my brain heal, and soon enough I would have those desires to bond with my baby. God willing, and the creek don't rise. Dr. Jean told me I had an issue with "shoulding" on myself. During our support group sessions, she pointed out that I was quick to say unhelpful statements such as:

"I *should* be better by now."

"I *should* be able to do more by now."

"I *shouldn't* have these kinds of thoughts."

She told me that instead of "should," I can choose either "can" or "will."

"I *will* be better one day."

"I *can* do one thing at a time."

"I *can* remind myself to think of good things."

Instead of telling myself I was a bad mom because I couldn't muster up loving feelings towards my daughter, I told myself that I can continue to do the work to help my brain heal. Maybe one day I will feel those feelings. Maybe not. I didn't think so.

* * *

Then we went on a real vacation.

I still didn't know if I was allowed such a luxury as a new mom. I knew friends who had two or more children and hadn't been on a vacation since before the eldest child's birth. It seemed like constant exhaustion and endless sacrifice was part of the mom gig. But Grandma Hardwick offered us three nights at her timeshare in the Great Smoky Mountains for free. Noah and I had visited the Smokies dozens of times over the course of our marriage. It was our happy place, with bears, beautiful views, and tacky T-shirt shops.

We planned to go the last weekend of August, and I began to grow fond of Lorelai as the month edged closer to vacation days. She had grown into a strong, smart, and healthy baby. Just like we prayed for every night during my pregnancy. I loved that I could see Noah's smile on her face. It was just as charming as his. She seemed frustrated at her inability to transport herself. She wanted to crawl, but she seemed irritated that she couldn't. She liked to roll from one corner of the room to the other. She cried less, but it was still her primary mode of communication.

She cried in the car and screamed in protest if I tried to walk her in the stroller. She loved to lay on her stomach and stretch her limbs and head up off the floor so she could look around and wiggle and learn.

Tulip seemed to be healed of her skin wounds after several rounds of antibiotics. We dropped her off along with Lorelai and a closet's worth of clothes, blankets, pacifiers, bottles, formula and dog food at Stephanie and Dan's house. Lorelai adhered to her schedule well, which I had written out in detail. I wanted to provide an instruction manual to ensure maximum enjoyment to all parties involved. I held Lorelai and tried to give her a lot of kisses. She protested, and wiggled ferociously for me to let her lay on the floor and roll around. She was ready for us to leave, and we left.

Noah and I loved the four-hour car ride in and of itself. It was deliciously quiet. We talked some, and then we listened to music and held hands. I was so thankful to have my husband all to myself. I told Noah I wanted to choose to not worry about Lorelai during vacation. I wanted to just enjoy the moment. He said it was an excellent plan.

> "Enjoy life with the wife whom you love,
> All the days of your vain life that he has given you under the sun,
> Because that is your portion in life and in your toil at which you toil under the sun."
> Ecclesiastes 9:9 (ESV)

The first full day of vacation was the second-best day of my life. The best day ever was my wedding day, but this was a close second. I woke up and drank coffee and painted on the porch. I had found painting to be extremely therapeutic, and when I coupled it with a quiet environment in nature, my creative soul nearly burst from joy. Then, because I could, I went on a walk. I waved at everyone I passed by and I could not stop smiling. I stopped to look at flowers. I took in the view of the Smokies. I assessed the surrounding miles and guessed where I would want to be if I were a bear. My goal for every trip to the Smokies has always been to see a bear.

I walked back to find Noah still asleep. I didn't want to wake him. I made myself breakfast and turned on the gas fireplace. It was late August in Tennessee, but I just really wanted to sit in front of the fireplace. Then I took a bath. Then I fell asleep on the couch. It was the second-best day of my life, and it was only 10:30 in the morning. Noah woke up and asked me what I wanted to do that day. I didn't move from the couch and responded, "I'm already doing what I want to do today. I want to do more of this."

He smiled and said that was fine by him. Eventually we rallied up enough energy to sit by the pool. We cooked dinner, I took my second bath of the day, and I went to bed early. The next day was similar, but we did venture outside of the timeshare property. We strolled down the road that passes through Gatlinburg. Most buildings had been burned in a fire in recent years, and we saw only a few of our old favorite posts. Fortunately, our favorite Mexican restaurant survived. They have the best salsa. Vacation salsa.

That was probably the third-best day of my life.

I didn't think about Lorelai. We called Stephanie every night to check in. Lorelai did her baby thing just as well at her grandparents' house than she did at her own home: sleep, bottle, pee, poop, cry a little, roll on the floor, etc. Lots of volume. Lots of bodily fluids. Stephanie said that she enjoyed Lorelai, but she forgot how hard it is to watch a small baby. Babies are hard, every one of them. There is no such thing as an *easy baby*.

On our last day of vacation, the fourth-best day of my life, we took a day trip to Asheville, North Carolina. It was another one of our favorite places to visit in our "old life." Pre-baby life. We walked up and down the streets, and ate at the restaurant we loved most from our prior visit. It was another Mexican restaurant, and they also had excellent salsa. We took our time, and we held hands. We looked at used bookstores and vintage clothing boutiques. We had a glass of wine in an open-air cafe, and we people-watched in a blissful shared silence.

The next day we drove home, and I was solemn. I wasn't excited to see Lorelai. I hadn't missed her, and I again couldn't decide if that was a good thing or a bad thing. Regardless, she needed me and vacation was over. My shoulders and back didn't hurt anymore after four days without the weight of a baby in my arms. I felt like I had caught up on sleep. I felt like I knew my husband again. I had read books and painted paintings and sat in the sun and in the bath. I was able to spend each morning on the porch with my Bible and my coffee and my Jesus. I felt like I had been able to recharge my batteries after spending so much time blinking red at 1%. I felt renewed and refreshed. We invested in our marriage, and we trusted Lorelai would benefit from that.

Our trip was a gift that I didn't even know I needed. I hadn't asked for it, but we were given it anyway. The Lord knew we needed to rest because that's the way He made us.

"Abide in me, and I in you.
As the branch cannot bear fruit by itself, unless it abides in the vine,
Neither can you, unless you abide in me.
I am the vine;
You are the branches.

Whoever abides in me and I in him, he it is that bears much fruit,
For apart from me you can do nothing."
John 15:4-5 (ESV).

CHAPTER 17
Fall

By the end of the summer, I thought that I would have had this whole postpartum depression thing behind me. I didn't. I had good days; I really did. Lorelai started to crawl around six months, and it improved her mood drastically. She was clearly happy with herself that she was mobile. I felt I was beginning to bond with her. Finally. I became more affectionate with her. We read books constantly. She still hated rides in the car, and protested loudly. But I could sense my heart finally beginning to melt. To open up to my daughter.

To me, that was a miracle.

One week before Lorelai turned 6 months old, I posted this picture on social media, with the below caption.

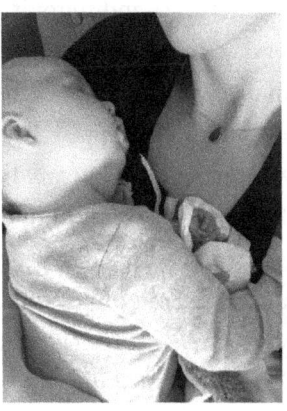

"Healing happens! I didn't get enough of these sweet moments when she was a freshie out of the oven. Too much sickness, mentally and physically, stood in the way. It's painful to think about. The thing is, becoming attached to my nugget just happened on a different timeline than some others. It's all good, though! We trust in the promise that 'the old has passed and the new has come*'! Thank you, Jesus, for healing and hope and restoration!"

*2 Corinthians 5:17

Every day I made myself get out and attempt to be productive with Lorelai. I knew I needed the structure. Whether it be a "playdate" at a friend's house, a trip to the grocery store together, or a workout at the gym with her beside me in her stroller, I knew I had to have a focus every day. I needed a reason to take a shower. I needed to see people my own age and have adult conversations. I made it a rule for myself. I had to do "one thing" every day outside of the apartment. Other than that, I was still unbearably exhausted. It wasn't a sleep-deprived type of exhaustion anymore. It was heavy and oppressive. Like my body was weighed down and squeezed tight and emptied.

So tired.

Tulip's skin condition had returned, and it took over her body. Large sores formed from her nose to her tail, almost overnight. We had to shave all of her hair off. The veterinarian cultured her skin, and we found out it was a staph infection. She didn't want to eat or play. She started a fourth round of antibiotics and steroids and required a medicated bath every other day. To me, it was torture. I would bathe her and soak the sores in medicated shampoo, then I would wrap her in a clean cotton blanket until she stopped shaking. She was now more expensive than we could afford, but we didn't know what to do. Our cars broke down within a month of each other and we couldn't afford it. The hospital bills had wiped out our checking account, our savings, and maxed out our credit card.

I was still a nervous wreck every single night. It never failed that at 8:00 p.m. my body started running on some different fuel than it did during the daytime. It was overwhelming. It was a panic attack every night for an hour or more. The best thing I could do was to sit with Noah and focus on deep breathing, prayer, and distract myself until it was over. Sometimes I did that. The worst thing I could do was drink and watch TV in the dark to try to escape. Sometimes I did that. I dreaded the night time, but I couldn't explain to other people why. No one else I knew had timely meltdowns every day.

I still cried every day. I struggled to make decisions. Even simple questions like, "what do you want to eat for dinner?" were overwhelming at times. I couldn't focus on much of anything. During an appointment with Dr. S., she told me that these were the remaining symptoms of postpartum depression. I thought it was just how my life looked as a mother. I thought it was my new normal. Dr. S. then prescribed me 150 mg of Wellbutrin and increased my Zoloft prescription to 200 mg. I told her I didn't want to be dependent on any more medication. Then she told me something I needed to hear, even if it hurt.

She told me the addition of medication wasn't just about me. It was about Lorelai. She was right.

If I continued to live with severe depression, it would inevitably affect my child in a negative way. She needed a healthy mother. That realization was a turning point for me and my attitude towards treatment. I could see I was no longer in crisis mode, but I still had a long road to travel. It was up to me to give Lorelai a healthy home. She was totally innocent in the situation and she deserved the best of me. I had to continue to work.

Dr. S. and I talked through the 8:00 p.m. trigger, and we connected it to the time my induction was scheduled to begin. 8:00 p.m. It was a significant time. It was when everything started. It marked the beginning of trauma. I told Dr. S. that I thought traumatic experiences were limited to wars or physical violence or sexual assault. I didn't think childbirth could be considered traumatic. She explained that trauma can happen in all sorts of scenarios. I legitimately feared for my life on more than one occasion since 8:00 p.m. on March 15th.

Dr. S. referred me to a group of physicians in downtown Cincinnati who specialize in the treatment of PTSD. She advised that we needed to explore the possibility of a PTSD diagnosis since I still experienced nightly panic episodes. She asked if I experienced dreams or flashbacks in addition, and I said yes. I hadn't realized that was not a normal thing after giving birth. I told her that I was afraid of pregnancy. I said I was afraid to relive the situation. I believed it could happen again, even though it wasn't rational. It was as if my brain had healed and recovered at a faster rate than the rest of my body. My body remembered everything, even though my brain was beginning to forget.

I agreed to the increase in Zoloft and the addition of Wellbutrin. By the end of the appointment, Lorelai was in a fuss. I always brought her with me, as usual. Dr. S asked me if I had any childcare options.

"I am a 'stay-at-home-mom', and I don't have the extra money for childcare," I explained.

Noah and I decided this was the setup we wanted for our family. I would stay home full time and he would work. She told me I couldn't afford *not to* set up regular child care. She told me I needed to have time to myself so that I could go, for instance, to one of my many doctor appointments without distraction. I had to get regular relief from taking care of a baby. She said that even though Noah was available to help with Lorelai weekday nights and weekends, it was obviously not enough for me. I needed more help. I was still sick, and I could not get better on my own.

I had to humble myself enough to admit I needed more help. It wasn't an easy pill to swallow, but I knew it was the truth. It was the way God designed me. It didn't matter if I saw other moms who *seemed* to "have it together." I did not have it together, and that was O.K. I could do nothing on my own.

> "Two people are better off than one, for they can help each other succeed.
> If one person falls, the other can reach out and help.
> But someone who falls alone is in real trouble."
> Ecclesiastes 4:9-10

I got serious about recovery. The clock was ticking. Lorelai watched everything I did with endless curiosity, and I knew she was smart. I wanted to give her the best role model I could. I wanted to show her what a healthy mommy looks like. Now, it was not about me, it was about *us*.

The Wellbutrin gave me energy to pursue some things other than laying on the floor in a dark room, so Dr. S. increased the dose to 300 mg. I had forgotten what it felt like to have energy. I cut out gluten for a week as an experiment. My brain fog began to clear up in three days. I didn't even know I had fog in my brain until I felt what it was like to have clear sunshine there. It made a difference. I pursued hormone therapy, and I was prescribed bioidentical progesterone along with a mixture of vitamins and supplements. Vitamin D, Fish Oil, probiotics, an adrenal support, B-vitamins, CBD oil, and a holistic sleep-aid remedy.

My body needed to be rebuilt. There was a lot of restoration to do.

Noah and I began to date again. Crisis mode was over. We needed to get to know each other all over again. It was the best thing for our whole family. Stephanie and Dan helped to watch

Lorelai for those blissful few hours of freedom. It didn't matter what we did, it could be as simple as a cup of coffee together. We were Mr. and Mrs., by ourselves, and it made us giddy. I still couldn't stay out after 8:00 p.m., unless I wanted to experience a complete and total meltdown in public, which happened once or twice. I still spent my late evenings in panic.

• • •

I went through a screening process for PTSD. I learned that this disorder can result after a person experiences or witnesses a terrifying event. For me, the agony of a difficult labor, the dangerous infection that developed, and the following weeks of violent gastrointestinal distress had messed with the hardwiring of my brain. The doctors at the practice reviewed my file and together came to an agreement that my situation did not fit all the criteria required for a PTSD diagnosis. There was no specific moment where I feared for my life. Rather, it was a series of terrifying experiences, but not specific enough to warrant a diagnosis.

Dr. S then said that I needed to pursue individual therapy. I reminded her that I already finished the support group commitment. 12 weeks. Wasn't that enough? Didn't I graduate from that?

Apparently not.

I made an appointment to talk with Dr. Jean individually. I wanted to get better, and if that's what it would take, then that's what I would do.

Every Wednesday morning during the fall, our church's "Mom's Group" met. The children were dropped off at childcare and we got to sit in a room and build our village. We shared our struggles, which all had uncanny similarities, perhaps because we were all in the parent-of-a-small-child phase. There were half a dozen "mentor moms" who had survived to see their children reach adulthood. They had experience, and I didn't. I wanted to hear from people who had walked the same path I found myself on, but they were a couple miles farther down the road.

I heard stories of grace and pain and everything in between. We all wanted to raise our children to love Jesus. We were all in this together. It was messy, and it was good. I enjoyed those two hours of nearly-free childcare. I knew and trusted the ladies who watched Lorelai, and she did too. The childcare workers were well intentioned when they told me that she did so well with people other than myself. They said she was an easy baby, that "she didn't seem to mind if I came or went!" I smiled and said thank you, but I also wondered if this was because she had spent so much time alone when she was so young. I couldn't be at her beck and call because I was so sick and much of the time stuck in the bathroom. She was used to having to wait for me.

We also arranged for Lorelai to be watched four hours every week. It was expensive, and we couldn't really afford it. Still, it was worth it. I got so much done during those four hours without a baby. Dr. S. was right, regular childcare helped my mental state. It was something I could look forward to. It gave me the opportunity to invest in the parts of me that were not *mommy*. It broke up the monotony of the crying, and the crying, and the feeding, and the diapers, and the crying. I hated the crying.

Recovery wasn't streamlined or immediate, as I hoped it would be. But I could look back and see how far I had come, and it gave me the motivation to continue. I knew I never had to be alone. Before I had Lorelai, I envisioned myself doing it all. I would raise the baby, cook the food, delight my husband, care for our home and do it all with ease. I was so wrong. So wrong. But that's O.K. I stopped calling myself "a planner." I stopped envisioning the future, because I realized my expectations generally do not match reality. One day at a time I lost a bit more of that gnawing desire to control every aspect of my life. It was good.

I no longer wished for a quick fix or a pill that would take all the pain away. I came to realize that my recovery was my own, on my own time. Medication hadn't brought complete healing, but it helped. The support group hadn't brought complete healing, but it helped. Holistic medicine hadn't brought complete healing, but it helped. The more resources I was able to use, the more it helped. God was in the process of miraculous healing, and it wasn't because of anything I did. It took a village to put this mother back together again.

I focused on one aspect of the future: that it would be for my good. I didn't generally *feel* good, and I didn't necessarily *feel* hopeful, but I knew the truth and that is the rock I clung to.

"And we know that for those who love God all things work together for good,
For those who are called according to his purpose."
Romans 8:28 (ESV)

In late November, when Lorelai was eight months old, we moved to a different apartment. Our current apartment was a twenty- or thirty-minute commute depending on traffic. As a mom with a small child, I wanted that extra half an hour a day with Noah. I didn't see the apartment before we moved. My requirements were few: no increase in the rent payment, an extra bedroom, and on the first floor. Noah found a two-bedroom apartment on the first floor in a community only five minutes from his work. I told him to sign me up, no questions asked. This was our eighth move in ten years of marriage, and I trusted his opinion. Lorelai made it difficult to pack, and I tossed a lot of things in the donation box or the trash bin. I just wanted to get it over with, and I didn't want to bring anything we didn't need.

I took a photograph of our last night in our old apartment. I wanted to remember it, and I wanted to always appreciate the addition of more room. We had enough space, but God gave us more. Instead of sleeping next to the kitchen table, Lorelai could sleep in a bedroom of her own. It was a luxury, and we were thankful. Noah and I had gotten used to money and fancy apartments before we came to Ohio. Then the Lord humbled us for the eighteen months we lived in Stephanie and Dan's basement. We learned how much better it is to have little with love than to have much with hearts full of sadness. The first day at our new apartment felt like a vacation in a luxury hotel. It was quiet and had lots of trees and lakes and walking trails. Lorelai crawled up and down the long hallway with a contagious enthusiasm. It seemed huge, and the sensation of closing her bedroom door when she went to sleep was magnificent. It was a new place without bad memories.

It was a fresh start.

"Better is a little with the fear of the Lord
Than great treasure and trouble with it."
Proverbs 15:16 (ESV)

CHAPTER 18
Christmas

Baby's First Christmas.

I knew it was special. Lorelai wouldn't remember it, but I certainly wanted to. The one Christmas tradition I loved was with Noah: funny Christmas pictures. Every year we picked a silly theme, and we went all out for funny satirical Christmas cards that delighted our friends and confused our grandparents. We even had alternate identities during our Christmas photos: Chester and Vivian VonHardwick. It was our sixth year to honor the tradition, but this time we had Lorelai. Expectations were high. That year we picked the theme "flower children." Noah and I always put a lot of thought into the costumes, and this year we needed three. It was one of our first big creative projects since we became parents, and the pressure was on. It was ridiculous, and I loved it.

We showed up to the outdoor photo shoot with the photographer, and I laughed. I laughed and I laughed and I laughed because we looked as ridiculous as always, and Lorelai had no choice but to comply with her silly parents. When the photos were done, I laughed more. When I saw our family doing something we do well, have fun, I was proud of us. I was proud of Lorelai. I was proud of myself. It was a glimpse of the real me coming back. The me who liked to laugh and make a joke about most everything. These silly pictures were a sign of victory, that I was not just a depressed patient anymore. I was still *me*.

Lorelai and I began to form a deep bond. It was indescribable. I wanted to hold her. I wanted to give her kisses and hugs and gentleness. I wasn't afraid of her anymore. I fell in love. I was so proud of her for who she had become. I began to tell her the same three things every day. At first, I wasn't able to put much heart into it, but I knew if I spoke the same words day in and day out that they would grow into something solid and eternal. I knew the power of words. I looked her in the eyes each day and said:

"I love you for who you are on the inside.

I am proud of you for who you are on the inside.

You are my gift from God."

• • •

She still didn't *feel* like a gift, but I *knew* she was one. More importantly, I wanted her to know that she is a gift, not a burden. I wanted her to have these words ingrained in her heart and her mind so she would have no doubt that she was loved wherever she ended up in life. I knew I couldn't make up for any lost time. I knew our relationship had started later than most, but because of that it became so special. It was sacred. I wanted to protect it and nourish it. It was a love unimaginable. I tasted sweetness, and it took over. I wanted to tell everyone about it.

She was amazing.

I was able to create a nursery for her with our new apartment. I chose the theme "A Midsummer Night's Dream." Ethereal and elegant. I hung up yards of green garland and pink flowers and art and draped silk ribbons. Lorelai had a bookshelf and boxes of plush animals and colorful toys, all of which were gifts, most of which came from her grandparents. I wanted her bedroom to be her special space where she could learn and rest and flourish. We finally put her crib together, and she loved to snuggle in it with her soft blankets and silk lovie animals. My heart had changed fast, and I couldn't even believe it. I couldn't believe I saw my daughter for who she truly is. The scales on my eyes from the postpartum depression had begun to fall off, and there was no turning back.

JOURNAL ENTRY: DECEMBER 18
Christmas is one week away! I have no presents, no tree, no preparation, and a full heart. Father, Son, and Holy Spirit — be in our home, an overwhelming presence like the star in Bethlehem. The promise is being met in your perfect and good timing. Be near Jesus, Merciful King. Protect me, a slave to your love. Be near Jesus, come quickly.

DECEMBER 24

This Christmas season,
> No tree is up.
> No stockings hung.
> We spent $3.50 for gifts on each person at the Dollar tree.
> Best. Christmas. Ever.
> For reals. Just being together. I'm thankful.
> I have a brain to think thoughts-
> Thank you, God.
> I have hands to work —
> Thank you, God.
> I love my husband —
> Thank you, God.
> I have a healthy baby —
> Thank you, God.

On Christmas morning we drove north to see Noah's step dad's side of the family. Grandma cooked the same incredible food that she does every year. We sat around their big dining room table, and Lorelai sat on my lap. There were eleven of us, and it was a wonderful opportunity to introduce Lorelai to the same tradition I had come to love. It was comfortable and secure. We shared a plate of food, and she loved everything. She was already quite a gourmand and ate with an endearing enthusiasm.

When it was time to open presents, Lorelai and her new baby cousin were the stars of the show. They crawled together over the pile of packages, and everybody laughed. They didn't know how to open the paper or the bags, but each of them liked to pick the colorful bows off of the packages one by one. Lorelai wore the Christmas dress my mom had sent for her. It was made with white tulle and gold polka dots, and she looked like one of the angels that could top the tree.

That was a good moment.

* * *

We went home to take an afternoon family nap. We started this tradition every Sunday afternoon, to rest together. Lorelai slept in her bedroom, and we slept in our bedroom. Tulip snuggled under the blankets. She was still covered in sores and on her sixth round of antibiotics. We prayed for her to be healed, but it didn't look promising. We all slept in a blissful Christmas silence. Anytime I was able to sleep, I was thankful to the Lord for that gift. I knew I needed rest to have a healthy mind. A nap can be a holy act of surrender. Even Jesus took naps.

> "One hand full of rest is better than two fists full of labor and striving after the wind."
> Ecclesiastes 5:6 (NASB)

That evening, we drove west to see Noah's mom's side of the family. Stephanie and her mother had cooked our traditional Mexican Christmas dinner: enchiladas, tamales, chili rellenos, and homemade salsa which went well with everything. It was delicious. Lorelai tried everything, but her favorite was the enchilada with the soft corn tortilla and perfectly seasoned meat. Someone had put a red bow on the top of her head, and she looked so happy. She clapped and smiled, and I just took it all in. Christmas. With *my* daughter. We had made it to this milestone, and it was worth celebrating.

We drove home, and Lorelai fell asleep in the car. Noah and I were both exhausted, but it was a good type of tired. I still had my usual 8:00 p.m. nervous breakdown, but I had experienced a full day before it hit me. I had lived a whole day as myself.

I was able to talk to my family and make memories and engage in the moment. I was able to soak it in. I thanked the Lord for the miracle of the day. We celebrated Christmas because His promises were fulfilled through the birth of his Son. Jesus. The healer. The mender of my heart and my body. The life and the light and the joy. I celebrated because I lived a miracle life. He had given me a whole new start.

> "Therefore, if anyone is in Christ,
> The new creation has come:
> The old has gone,
> The new is here!"
> 2 Corinthians 5:17 (NIV)

Journal entry from December 31:

LAST DAY OF THE YEAR.

Dear sweet Lord, thank you for your life breathing miracles this year to bring me to this place. I feel honored and humbled, equally, to be shown such magnificent grace.

Lord God I just still feel like a child trying to pretend to be a functioning adult.

I love Lorelai. God, thank you for making her great and sleepy and healthy and strong and smart and a world changer for the Gospel.

Nobody knows my heart but you, Lord.

No one sees my thoughts but you.

What do you think of me?

I love you, Lord. You are faithful. You never fail. You are constant in grace. Your eyes show mercy.

Father, Son, Holy Spirit: my specific prayer for today, the last day of the year, is that you will give me wisdom and forgiveness.

CHAPTER 19
Spring

January and February were hard, but they are always hard. It's cold and dark. Dr. S. told me that a light box could help, so I sat in front of mine for an hour or more every day. The bright light's frequency mimics the real sun and helps the body to make more Vitamin D. It helped, but it was still cold and dark. I was nauseated from the combination of 200 mg of Zoloft and 300 mg of Wellbutrin every morning, but they helped. I went to "Mom's Group" every week. I wrote every day. I meditated, I prayed, and I slept because it helped. I exercised and talked to adults because it helped. I had arrived at a place where I was not hesitant to ask for help.

I knew my limits. By then, I knew I was created to need a lot of help.

We all are.

Lorelai became chatty, even though she didn't speak English. I talked to her constantly. Our bond became deeper as each day passed. I couldn't believe it. It was a miracle. I adored her. She was fearless and tough. She didn't laugh easily, but she had a good sense of humor, nonetheless. I could tell. She made friends with everyone, just like Noah. She had his smile, and it made me melt. God gifted her with incredible health, even though she hadn't had much breastmilk. God took care of her health regardless of what my body could or could not do. I knew I had made the right choice for our family to stop nursing when I did. We were all still alive, which meant success.

The depression had continued to lift ever so slightly each day, and I could think clearly again. For the most part. I continued to panic each night, but Dr. Jean and I began to meet once a month to deal with the fears. I was afraid I would have to experience the same first month postpartum again, even though it wasn't a rational thought. I was afraid I would have to endure the same thirty-one-hour labor, even though I knew logically it was impossible. I hadn't thought about killing myself in a while, but it still happened sometimes. Satan continued to lie, but the Lord had equipped me to recognize the lies and battle them with His Scripture. I had to be on the offensive.

It was war.

"For though we live in the world, we do not wage war as the world does.
The weapons we fight with are not the weapons of the world.
On the contrary, they have divine power to demolish strongholds.
We demolish arguments and every pretension that sets itself up against the knowledge of God,
And we take captive every thought to make it obedient to Christ."
2 Corinthians 3-5 (NLT)

We went into credit card debt, and it was stressful. We paid over ten thousand dollars to the hospital for the medical expenses, and we couldn't seem to recover from it. That was in addition to the health insurance premiums that cost eight-hundred dollars per month. God continued to provide, as He always does. He always has, and He always will. We couldn't afford to be parents, but God math made it work. If I went back to work full-time, the vast majority of the income would go towards childcare. It wasn't what we wanted for our family.

God provided our daily bread.

I continued to build support within this new *mommy* stage of life. In the past when I worked, I made friends with coworkers. When I went to school, I made friends with other students. But now? If I wanted to have friends, I had to go out and make it happen. I love my daughter, but I've never wanted to be her best friend. I tried to have her around other kids her own size as often as I could. "Mom's Group" and church provided childcare, and each Friday she played with her cousin. Lorelai spoke baby, not English, and I knew she needed little people who could understand her. I had a new desire for community and authenticity in my relationships. I had experienced true community in the past year, and I wanted more of it.

I needed my village.

"Let us think of ways to motivate one another to acts of love and good works.
And let us not neglect our meeting together,
As some people do,
But encourage one another, especially now that the day of his return is drawing near."
Hebrews 10:24-25 (NLT)

Jesus healed Tulip. It was miraculous. After nine rounds of antibiotics and medicated baths for the past six months, her wounds had healed. She wasn't in pain. She wanted to play again. The springtime brought life to her body and mine. I believe God knew that I really cared about that dog, and He healed her in His time. It was a gift for me. Lorelai laughed when she watched

Tulip play fetch with her tennis balls. She thought it was just hysterical, and her laugh was contagious.

We began to have dinner together as a family every day as Lorelai learned to incorporate more and more new foods and flavors into her life. Noah and I decided to make dinner at home a priority. We prayed before each meal, and Lorelai learned to wait to eat until we gave our thanks. I still couldn't believe I was given such beautiful moments. To sit and eat as a family. I didn't think I would live to see it, and I never thought I would be able to have a calm conversation over dinner again. It wasn't perfect, and many nights were messy, but something about eating dinner as a family gave me such satisfaction. We could celebrate that we survived another day by His grace.

My priorities had changed. Everything had changed. I was healthy, and I didn't take it for granted any more. Child birth had given me a respect for my body that I had lacked for so many years as a bulimic. Sometimes I ate too much, and sometimes I ate too little. Sometimes I exercised and energized my body, and sometimes I rested. I listened to my body with new ears. Mom ears. I wanted to raise a daughter who would respect her body, and I knew it was up to me to show her how. She watched everything.

I no longer fixated on the idea of buying a house, a new car, or a fancy vacation. They now seemed frivolous. I knew that our apartment was more than enough room for us for right now, and that was good enough for me. Maybe one day we would own a home. Maybe not. Either way was fine. We drove Noah to work every day and picked him up in the evening with our one car. A car was a luxury. Even though it was a five-minute commute, I knew those ten minutes of family time in the car would add up and create memories for Lorelai. And me.

I didn't lower my standards or expectations; I just didn't have that desire for *more* anymore. I was safe. I was healthy. My family was safe and healthy. The competition-driven, achievement-oriented, status-searcher in me had died. She was gone. I was liberated. I was *good enough*, not because of anything I had achieved as a mother or wife or employee, but because of the Jesus who lived in my heart. I couldn't help myself, just like Lorelai couldn't change her own dirty diaper. I couldn't change myself, but God did. I couldn't provide for myself, but God did. I didn't need anything more.

On March 12, five days before Lorelai's first birthday, I wrote:

Father, Son, and Holy Spirit —

Be gentle and quick to forgive me, a sinner. Be gentle to me Lord as I learn to be gentle with myself.

You do the speaking. I have one mouth.

Help me to listen well — to listen without words, to see people's hearts.

Give me wisdom, Lord. Wisdom to care for Lorelai today. Wisdom as a wife.

To Tulip, to my neighbors.

I am empty, Lord, fill me with the power of the Holy Spirit.

For Lorelai's first birthday, I made her a quilt from her onesies that she had grown out of. I don't sew, but I can follow a straight line *most* of the time. It was good enough. It had asymmetry and messy stitches, but I liked it. A year ago, I wouldn't have liked it. I would have focused on the mistakes I had made and stuck it in the back of a drawer. I wouldn't want to show it to anyone, lest they be a legitimate sewer and laugh at my attempts to make straight corners. I would have been too focused on the quilt's appearance, and it probably wouldn't even have a chance to live out its usefulness: to bring warmth. To comfort. To remind us of memories.

It's not about how it looks.

It's not about how I planned for it to look.

It's about Jesus.

"Looking at them, Jesus said,
'With people it is impossible, but not with God;
For all things are possible with God.'"
Mark 10:27 (NASB)

He was there the whole time. I was never alone. Even when I doubted my body's ability to endure, the Lord had already begun the process of restoration and healing. My doubt was outweighed by the sacrifice He made for me thousands of years ago. It wasn't about me. The church had been His hands and feet for my family. He had worked through doctors and medicines. In the words of Grandma Hardwick, "If God can talk through a donkey, He can talk through a doctor. He can do anything He wants." He worked through nurses and hot meals and shared tears. He never stopped working.

Regardless of what I did or did not do as a mother, Lorelai was always God's child. He loved her more than I did. He loved her more than Noah did. She is my gift from Him, made special just for me. I can raise her as best as I can, but ultimately, she doesn't belong to me. She is His. She turned one year old on a Sunday. For her first birthday we didn't have a party. We didn't bake a cake. We went to church in the morning to praise God with our friends. We ate lunch with our family at El Corporal Mexican restaurant. They have good salsa. Lorelai opened her presents and put on her new hat with the price tag still intact like Minnie Pearl. It was so *us*.

A LIFE POSTPARTUM

• • •

This may not have been how I planned it, but it was good.

I used to boast in my strength, but now I was content to sit in my weakness. It brought a freedom I had not encountered before this year. Life would never be how I pictured it in my mind. There may be similarities, but God is in control. Not me. That means it's not my efforts or lack thereof that determine the future. It was determined long ago by a God who loved me and gave me new grace every day. Life would continue to be hard, but it wasn't hopeless. Jesus told us "here on earth you will have many trials and sorrows. But take heart, because I have overcome the world." (John 16:33, NLT). Yes, we will be broken-hearted, but we can take heart. We will lose battles, but Jesus gives us the victory. We will have loss and pain and sadness, but we know it will not last forever. We have each other. We have our daily bread. One day at a time we will carry each other's burdens, and together, we will build our village. In our weakness, we will find strength.

> "You have taught children and infants to tell of your strength,
> Silencing enemies and all who oppose you."
> Psalm 8:2 (NLT)

Where Are They Now?

Here we are. It's been over two years since Lorelai's birth, and I have been given a whole new life. My story has turned from desperation to celebration.

My mind has been restored. God took away my fear. I continued to work closely with my doctors well past my first year postpartum, because it takes a lot of time to break down trauma and flush it out for good. I had to go back to the worst moments of my story, face that fear, and deal with it head on until it no longer had any power over my mind. It took professional help and a lot of practice.

It was hard, and it was worth it.

My body has healed. It's strong. I've learned to treat it gently and give it the respect it has always deserved. This experience has taught me to see my body for what it can do, not how it looks. Now I get the opportunity to teach my daughter how to treat her body with this same respect, and it's powerful to watch.

That girl is going to move mountains.

I adore my sweet little lady Lorelai. She is very brave, and she inspires me to get back up when I fall down. She has learned how to find joy in any situation. Her voice is strong and rich, and she has a lot to say. God has given me this girl as a gift, and I tell her that every single day. Despite the challenges we faced together during her first year, we love each other deeply. Because of the challenges we faced together, our relationship is a treasure of gold refined by fire.

It's pure and beautiful.

Although I continue to take prescription medications as well as holistic supplements for my mental health, I know that medication is only one small part of a healthy lifestyle. I have to sleep enough, eat nutritious foods, exercise, rest, be aware of my mental state, ask for help when I need it, take a time out when things get crazy, and remind myself to just breathe.

If I don't take care of myself, I can't take care of my family.

I have learned to make time with God my number one priority. It has to be number one, or else I get so lost so quickly. Just like I feed my body every day, I have to feed my soul.

I also learned to make relationships my second priority. I need to be with my people so badly. All the time. I need to be loved and to show love, because that is what I was created to do. I could not have written this book without my people. I could not have made it to this point alone. I need them, and they need me too. It's just how we're made.

This year of 2020 has already brought the Covid-19 global pandemic, polarizing political rhetoric, and massive civil unrest as our country continues to battle racial injustice. The world is in chaos, but through Christ I am calm and at peace. While I've witnessed people grasp for any remaining sense of control over their lives, I've found rest in the knowledge that all control is an allusion. I never had it anyway, so I certainly haven't lost it.

I don't have time to worry about the details of the future because there are too many people who need to be loved today. That's my calling: to love without fear.

I know life is short. I know I could die at any moment, but

it's not something to worry about. If I die tonight, I know I will be with Jesus. Our economy may crash, but faith can stand. Our cities may burn but love never fails. In this time of social isolation, we still have each other.

Together, we can do anything. When we begin to share in each other's heartbreaks as well as each other's victories, we can build the type of village where everyone belongs.

We were never meant to live this life alone.

Faith

Maybe you've read my story and thought, "That's great her God got her through that situation. I don't have a God like that," or maybe, "I don't know that God." But maybe you want to. Maybe God is tugging at your heart to tell you that what you've been missing is HIM. A relationship with God doesn't immediately make everything better, as you could see from my story, but it does give everything HOPE. It gives us purpose and meaning beyond this life, which can be quite miserable sometimes. If you'd like to know this hope and peace, you simply need to tell the Lord.

Romans 10:9 says, "If you confess with your mouth, 'Jesus is Lord,' and believe in your heart God raised him from the dead, you will be saved."

That's it. It's that simple.

And yes, you will want to find a church and some Christian friends to help teach and walk alongside you. You'll also want to read the Bible so you can know God's will for you and learn to know Jesus as your best friend. The voice you'll learn to love the most will be His Holy Spirit who speaks to your heart and guides you into righteousness (John 16:8).

What are you waiting for? Start this journey today!

Resources

If you or someone you know struggles with postpartum depression or other mental health disorders, help is available now. The following resources are available anytime and anywhere in the U.S.A.:

National Crisis Text Line: text HOME to 741741

National Suicide Prevention Hotline and Website:
1-800-273-8255
www.suicidepreventionlifeline.org

Postpartum Support International Helpline and Website:
1-800-944-4773
www.postpartum.net

Substance Abuse and Mental Health Services Administration Helpline and Website:
1-800-662-4357
www.samhsa.gov

References

1. American Psychological Association. What is Postpartum Depression and Anxiety? [internet] https://www.apa.org/pi/women/resources/reports/postpartum-depression; Washington, DC. 2019.

2. CERVIDIL [package insert]. Parsippany, NJ: Ferring Pharmaceuticals Inc. 2. 2018 FDA Orange Book. https://www.accessdata.fda.gov/scripts/cder/ob/default.cfm. August 17, 2015.

3. Food and Drug Administration. Labeling of Infant Formula: Guidance for Industry. [internet] https://www.fda.gov/media/99701/download. Rockville, MD. September, 2016.

About the Author

Lisa grew up in Nashville, Tennessee and graduated *summa cum laude* from Middle Tennessee State University. She now lives in Ohio with her husband of twelve years, their two-year-old daughter, and eleven-year-old miniature schnauzer. During her journey through severe postpartum depression and postpartum anxiety, Lisa recognized the need to share her story in order to bring awareness to the subject, to break the stigma associated with these mental health disorders, and to shine a light for other mothers who feel alone in their suffering. Lisa is involved in faith-based groups in her local community which support and encourage new mothers, and she serves on the advisory board for the Women's Health Initiative Foundation.

www.ingramcontent.com/pod-product-compliance
Lightning Source LLC
Chambersburg PA
CBHW060530100426
42743CB00009B/1481